Standing Together

Standing
Together

women speak out about violence and abuse

edited by Linda Goyette

BRINDLE
&GLASS

Library and Archives Canada Cataloguing in Publication
Standing together : women speak out about violence and
abuse / edited by Linda Goyette.

ISBN 1-897142-11-0

1. Abused women. 2. Women—Violence against. I. Goyette, Linda,
1955–

HV6626.S72 2005   362.82'92   C2005-903645-1

Cover image: J. Alleyne Photography

Canada Council   Conseil des Arts
for the Arts   du Canada

Brindle & Glass is pleased to acknowledge the support of the Canada Council for the Arts
and the Alberta Foundation for the Arts for our publishing program.

The Alberta Council of Women's Shelters gratefully acknowledges the financial support of Alberta
Children's Services, Government of Alberta, for the Standing Together project.

Every effort has been made to obtain permission for quoted material. If there is an omission
or error the author and publisher would be grateful to be so informed.

Brindle & Glass Publishing
www.brindleandglass.com

Brindle & Glass is committed to protecting the environment and to the responsible use
of natural resources. This book is printed on 100% post-consumer recycled and
ancient-forest-friendly paper. For more information please visit www.oldgrowthfree.com.

1   2   3   4   5   08   07   06   05

PRINTED AND BOUND IN CANADA

"I know who I am. I am that woman who reached her breaking point, and after a good cry, I stood."
—Andrea Fikkert

⊞ ⊞ ⊞ ⊞

We honour the courage of all contributors to Standing Together*: the women who signed their full names to their stories and poems; those who used a pen name or chose anonymity to protect their identity; and those whose stories could not appear at all because of a threat to their safety. All stories and poems will be preserved.*

Contents

⌘ ⌘ ⌘ ⌘

Dedication

LORIE MISECK

This is for the woman who will not read this poem.
The one whose lidded eyes were once question marks.
The older sister, now younger.

This is for her
and the others like her
who've stood on the edge
of a landscape mapping a way in
and out.

For the woman in the alley bent over trash
whose address is her bones.
The woman in the park whose child stretches
her heart thin as toffee. The one under lamplight
packing small boxes so her husband won't notice
she's leaving.

This is for them
and the one so full of spring her bare hands
pull back soil to let her garden out.
The woman washing dishes and the one
plaiting her daughter's thick hair into
gold streams.

And this is for the woman who will not read this.
The one who hooked wool into landscapes,
reaching for rust, green and bleached blue sky.

This is for her
and the one whose eyes have turned to lemon seed
and must look away.
And for the one who won't.
This is for all of them.

For the woman baking bread, rising before sunlight,
letting the dog, scarred by time's impatience,
out and in and out again.
The one who won't trap the pregnant skunk
even though her night lawn is a ribbon
of black and white scent.

The woman whose hole in her breast is a moon
not a wound pressing near her heart.
For the old woman whose clothesline
once full of shirts and sheets
now holds only hers.

The grandmother whose hips are rusted hinges
yet moves across a room to take her daughter's hand.
For the mother who tells her daughter
she's a good mother.
For the mother who can't.
For the mother who won't.

This is for them, all of them
And for the woman who will not read this poem.
The one trapped in a photograph with sisters,
eyes breathing similar light, each reaching for
something beyond the lens, something unnamed
outside the frame.

Lorie Miseck lives in Edmonton with her husband, their two daughters, and two dogs. She has published two books: a poetry collection, the blue not seen *(Rowan Books, 1997), and a work of creative non-fiction,* A Promise of Salt *(Coteau Books, 2002), which won the Wilfred Eggleston Award for Non-Fiction. Lorie says she is pleased that "Dedication" opens this collection.*

I am a woman in Alberta, perhaps your daughter or sister, your mother or grandmother. I am your best friend in the world. I am a distant cousin. I am the newcomer in town.

I live in a high-rise apartment in downtown Edmonton; or on a cattle ranch in the foothills of the Rockies; or on a dairy farm in the Peace Country. I grew up on a Métis settlement near Lac La Biche; or near a military base at Cold Lake; or on a suburban street in Calgary. I am your neighbour in Medicine Hat or Grande Prairie; Fort Chipewyan or Pincher Creek; Crowsnest Pass or Fort McMurray; Slave Lake or the Siksika Nation; Edson or Rocky Mountain House; Lethbridge or Lloydminster; Stettler or the Saddle Lake First Nation; Wainwright or Big Valley. I moved here from a distant corner of Canada. I am an immigrant from Ethiopia or Chile, from China or Ukraine.

I am the receptionist in your office, or the cashier at your corner store. I am a successful businesswoman or a struggling artist; a high school student or a lab technician. I am the prostitute who stands on the corner at midnight. I am the nurse with three kids to raise. I am an addict in prison. I am a retired schoolteacher with grandchildren. I am 23. I am 50. I am 84. I am 37. I am 42. I am 17.

I saw a poster in the early winter of 2004. "Writers wanted," it said. "This book will celebrate the lives and experiences of women who have struggled with challenges, and yet live rich and joyful lives." The poster said the book would raise funds for the prevention of family violence and abuse across Alberta. It asked for stories and poems based on true events.

I sat down and wrote my story. It wasn't easy for me, but it is time I spoke for myself.

This is the first thing you need to know about me: I am stronger than you think. There are thousands of women in Alberta like me. It is our turn to tell you what happened to us, and why. We are standing together. Listen to us.

❈   ❈   ❈   ❈

Let Me Tell You How Bad It Was

⊠ ⊠ ⊠ ⊠

Measures

LESLIE WRAITHEN

Try to imagine crawling on your hands and knees under the windows, so he can't see that you are home. To be sure he can't see that you are packing up and leaving. Again.

Can you imagine spending a night in the bathroom, because it is the one room in your apartment that does not have a window? Imagine crawling to the kitchen for a snack in case he's watching from his car across the street. Imagine thinking to yourself you really should get a cordless phone—for times like these.

Can you see yourself waking up on the bathroom floor because your apartment is on the ground floor, and maybe he can get in? The bathroom door has a lock, and the bedroom door doesn't.

Imagine starting yet another new job. Imagine going into the office of your new boss with a photo, and saying, "This is a picture of the man who won't let me live my life. He will probably find me here. I will understand if you tell me I can't work here." Now imagine holding your breath and waiting for her to tell you that maybe it would be best if you found another place of employment.

Can you see yourself asking the grocery boy for help to the car, even though you have only one bag, because you know you've been followed to the store?

Picture yourself devising a system of one ring followed by two rings for people calling you, so you know when and when not to answer your phone. Because somehow he has found your number again, even though you are unlisted.

Can you imagine taking a self-defence course—not in case you are assaulted, but rather because you know you will be, sooner or later.

Imagine knowing that keeping your ugly little secret to yourself will probably land you in the hospital or worse. Now imagine swallowing your pride, and telling your ugly little secret to your bus driver, your banker, your dentist. Why your dentist? Because it is six months since you left him, and there he is: sitting in the waiting room when you arrive for your appointment.

Imagine informing your landlord and your nosy neighbour so that, if you are lucky, they will help you if they hear you call for help. Imagine telling them, and watching them look away. Imagine your nosy neighbour turning up her television when she knows you are in danger right next door.

Imagine your unborn child being in danger from her very own father.

Imagine cutting yourself off from your family and friends and everything you love. Imagine trying to contain the danger to just yourself.

Picture yourself moving your children in the middle of the night to another shelter because he has found you again.

Try to imagine making life beautiful for your children while you heal from three broken ribs.

Picture yourself thinking you would rather be dead than be hunted. Imagine being more afraid of life than death.

Can you see yourself as that woman ducking into the men's room at the mall because you see him, and you need to hide, and the closest hiding place is the men's bathroom? . . .

Imagine yourself falling to the floor exhausted from the run you have just made, getting away from him. Picture yourself staying in the same place on the floor for hours on end, crying, pleading with God for just one day of peace. Imagine trying to find the Tylenol for the pain in your side, but being unable because your eyes are swollen shut.

Imagine coming home and finding your picture slashed in pieces and nailed to your front door. You live in a secured building, and you know he has been there. Who do you trust?

Envision a cab driver ringing your bell. Would you believe he has dropped by to make sure you are okay, because he was the one who picked you up last night when he saw you at the bus stop, hiding behind the bench? He didn't charge you for the fare. Now he is here to see if you need a ride to the hospital for the cut over your right eye and because your jaw looks broken. Imagine thanking him, and sending him away. You don't know his name and you never see him again.

What measures would you take to have your freedom in a free, democratic country? What measures would you take to survive when you are being stalked?

To what lengths would you go to protect your children when all the law can do is issue a restraining order—and when you know full well that this piece of paper will only act as kindling to the fire of his wrath?

What skills would you learn if you found yourself being hunted? How far would you go for a life of your own? Would you leave? Would you change the colour of your hair? Would you try to think like *him* so you could anticipate his next move?

What measures would you take if someone you knew was in this kind of danger, or had experienced even one of these things?

Would you help?

Leslie Wraithen is the pen name of an office administrator in the Edmonton area. She writes as a hobby, "to maintain a consistent cheerfulness, and to nurture some level of wisdom." Leslie says she emerged from an abusive relationship as an empowered woman with a choice about her future. She hopes to "evoke dreams, move mountains, awaken the inner thinker who has drifted off, inspire, and bring you to tears." She says she believes laughter is essential to basic survival.

❁ ❁ ❁ ❁

A Father Knows Best Kind of Life
DOLLY DENNIS

Here is the memory.

It is raining. Night. I am helping my younger brother and mother carry what little we own, walking ten blocks to our new walk-up apartment. We have to move quickly in case he appears. I know he won't, because he is a security guard on the night shift and has just left for work.

The night before, I had finally stood up to him, shouting, "Leave her alone!" as he was about to strike my mother again with his hand. I had surprised myself. Was that my voice? I waited for him to undo his belt and whip me as he had always done, but instead my father stared at me, stunned, as though he had just witnessed an apparition of the Blessed

Virgin Mary. It was the first time I had ever talked back to him.

I was eighteen, just graduated from secretarial school, and about to start my first job as a secretary. I could now take care of my brother and mother, get them away from the beast—because my mother was too afraid, embarrassed, to do anything—and besides, where would we go? It was 1965 and there were no women's shelters to embrace us.

That night I was in too much of a hurry to remember to cry. . . . Just get us out of here. I never looked back at that pink stucco house until fifteen years later, when I gave my husband a tour of my childhood. As we passed the two-storey building, I remember shaking uncontrollably until it was finally out of sight. "Go fast," I anxiously whispered.

The house had been converted into several apartment suites. My family occupied the upper unit in the back—a kitchen, living room, one bedroom, a shared bathroom in the hallway, and a closed-in back porch—thirty-five dollars a month. My brother slept in the living room on the couch, while I slept on a roll-up bed on the porch. In summer I welcomed the cool breeze blowing through the screen door, but in winter I froze. No amount of stuffing towels to fill in the cracks and crevices could warm that porch. To this day I am immune to cold weather.

I have forgotten large chunks of my childhood, but what I do remember flashes by like scenes from a movie.

Scene 1
She is six years old and taking a bath when he comes at her with the remnants of a clothesline, whipping her tiny water-soaked body until the skin swells with red welts. She had been late coming home from the playground.

Scene 2
She cowers in the basement with her mother and brother, hiding under the steps with the rats until he leaves for work. He is on a rampage again, and they fear for their lives. She is eight.

Scene 3
She stays after school or sits on the stoop in front of her house, waiting for her mother to return from her bakery job. She is afraid to be alone with him. She is ten.

Scene 4

Her mother is laid off from her bakery job and there is no money. He makes his children drink a cup of Mazola oil to sustain them. The cupboard is bare.

Scene 5

She no longer enters the kitchen unless her mother or brother is there. If she does venture in, he playfully grabs her crotch, then pummels her against the wall with his body, touching her in places a father has no right to go. She is thirteen.

And this one . . .

Scene 6

Her parents are arguing. He is dressed in his Pinkerton security guard uniform. In his hand he clutches a brown paper bag stained from sandwiches ripe with tomatoes and mayonnaise. He was just about to leave for work when words got in the way. Suddenly he explodes, smashing his lunch bag against the living room wall, the tomatoes and mayonnaise dripping, splattering—the wall a Pollack painting. He is now chasing her mother into the kitchen. The little girl is catatonic, fixated on the scene in the kitchen, watching her mother cry out, "Jesus, Jesus, Jesus." Her father convulses on the linoleum floor, feet kicking, knees bent, his Pinkerton revolver pointed to his head.

She watches *Father Knows Best* and dreams of having a father like the one on television. Please Lord, she prays, all I want is a normal life.

In 1980 my mother called to say my father was in the hospital, dying, and did I want to see him. This man, who had spent a lifetime yelling and screaming at his family, was finally silenced—the surgeons had cut out his tongue to arrest the cancer growing inside his throat. And I cried. Not for him, but for the little girl who never had a father, never knew, never would know, a father's love, never would feel his warmth or strength, or hear him say, "You are my beautiful little girl and I will protect you." It is from a father that a daughter develops a sense of herself as a woman.

And so, I spent the rest of my life trying to find this woman, recover my lost self-esteem and self-worth. I grew up believing I was a failure, a whore, a bastard child, an incompetent human being not fit to walk the earth. I might as well be dead. What good was I?

People ask me how it is that I turned out so "normal." I could have easily taken another path, rebelled, become a delinquent and proven my father right. What saved me were my dreams, which were born from people who touched me at important moments in my life: a Grade 9 teacher who read my English compositions out loud to the class and told me I should be a writer; an art teacher who said I should be an artist; a school friend who took pleasure inviting me to her home, and showed me a different side of family life, and that all fathers were not like mine. I envied her because she had one of those *Father Knows Best* types of dads.

I also read a lot—self-analysis books to overcome my shyness, psychological books to understand my childhood, etiquette books to regain my self-confidence, autobiographies to find role models. And I wrote—songs, poems, journals, plays, and short stories. I purged my soul, and found me. It takes a lifetime to undo the wrongs done to a child. It takes a lifetime to finally say, "Yes, I'm one terrific lady. I'm going to be okay."

I tell people to move on and not dwell on the past, to live in the moment, to have hope, and to expect nothing. It is the hardest thing to do—much easier to take solace in a bottle of vodka, or swallow some pills to escape whatever life has thrown. I struggle every day, but I refuse to become a victim, or blame failings on an abusive childhood. And I tell people to allow themselves time to mourn and cry at life's losses—but only for a day. Stay in bed, draw the drapes, weep, sleep, weep. Then get over it. We're survivors. We will all feel pain, fear; we will all know death and sickness; we will all experience some adversity in our lives. Life is courage and bravado. It isn't easy. Death is.

The other day, the TV show *Dateline* profiled a mother who was imprisoned for killing her two adult sons to spare them from the agony of Huntington's. She had previously nursed her husband and mother-in-law, and watched them slowly die from this horrific disease. Unable to contain herself, she honoured her sons' wishes and ended their suffering—suffocating them as they slept. I wept at her courage and wondered if I could have had the strength to deal with her struggles. My tragic childhood seemed so trivial in comparison, and yet pain is pain. It has become almost a cliché, but we are truly only given what we can bear.

It has taken me a lifetime to feel good about myself. At fifty-six I finally have my *Fathers Knows Best* kind of life—a husband who thinks I'm beautiful and talented, and an eighteen-year-old son who thinks there is no one else like me in the world. It has taken me a lifetime to understand that I make my life what I want it to be—I am the boss of me!

> ❖ *Dolly Dennis, an Edmonton writer originally from Montreal, has worked as a secretary, actress, dancer, and playwright. Since moving to Alberta in 1993, she has had her short stories published in* Other Voices *and* A Room of One's Own. *She is a recent winner in* CBC *Radio's Alberta Anthology writing competition.*
>
> *"I struggled as I revisited some of those childhood secrets that now appeared on my computer screen," she writes. "I wondered if I would have the courage to submit it, but here it is. Do as you please. Perhaps my experience will help someone else. It is one of the reasons I write—to make a difference."*

❖   ❖   ❖   ❖

I Never Look Back

COLLEEN KLEIN

The life of a man is a circle from childhood to childhood
And so it is in everything where power moves.

—Native American proverb

My journey into bullying, discrimination, and, eventually, family violence, began the day I was born.

I was born with a large birthmark that covers both sides of my face and extends down my neck. Up to the age of six, I lived with my great-grandparents on a ranch in the Cariboo Mountains of British Columbia.

I was isolated from other children and, as a result, had not yet experienced any discrimination or bullying.

My life changed when I entered school. The most common name I remember being called was "Indian red face." At the time, I didn't know about my Aboriginal heritage, so the name-calling was very confusing to me. I was a very hot-tempered child and I simply attacked my tormentors. They only picked on me once.

I married my first husband at the young age of sixteen to escape my father. I felt he questioned my honesty and integrity, and I just couldn't live with it. There is nothing worse in life than being falsely accused. As an adult I can see that he did the best he could as a father, and was a product of the way he was raised.

We eloped to Winnipeg and were married in 1957. I would wake up every morning before my husband so I could apply makeup to cover my birthmark, but one morning I didn't get up in time. He looked over at me in bed and saw the port wine birthmark, and his reaction was horrible. He yelled at me that I should have told him about it and that I was lucky to have him, as no other man would want me. I was crushed. I had no one to turn to, certainly not my parents, as I had already disappointed them by running away. I knew I had made the biggest mistake of my life, but my pride kept me from telling them. I just didn't want them to know I had made such a big mistake.

We moved to Calgary, where my husband was posted with the Canadian army. The violence started shortly after we settled in. He had a German Luger gun, which he kept in our suite. When he drank, he would become enraged and then lash out at the only person there he could unleash his anger on. He pointed the gun at me for hours at a time. My pride was still the only thing that kept me from leaving.

Three years after we married, I gave birth to the first of our two daughters. By this time, I was locked into the relationship by a sense of commitment to our child and by not wanting my father to know I had made a mistake. I had no one to talk to about the situation.

The violence began to occur on a regular basis. When he didn't use the gun, he used his fists, and I experienced cracked ribs and all the other injuries battered women receive. On one occasion, when I ended up with cracked ribs, his friend who was staying with us took me to the hospital. I told him that I was going to lay charges, but he told me that if I did, my husband would hunt me down and get even. I was afraid for my child and myself, so I did nothing.

The worst and most memorable attack on me occurred when our daughter was about five years old. We had rented a little house and he had set up a business. I was a stay-at-home mom and did the company books out of our house. One night, he came home drunk and started in on the verbal assaults. Eventually he brought out a loaded rifle. I was more terrified than I had ever been, more for my daughter than for myself. I was in bed, and my daughter was asleep in her room. He grabbed a pillow and sat on top of my chest with the rifle pointed at me through the pillow, pinning me so I couldn't move. It seemed like he kept me there for hours. At one point my little girl came in and asked him what he was doing. He said he was "playing cowboys with Mommy." Her presence distracted him and he left for a moment to go to the bathroom.

I had to make a split-second decision. Do I leave my daughter in her bedroom and run next door to call the police? Do I take her with me? Will he come out of the bathroom and shoot me? It was absolutely terrifying. I felt he would not hurt our daughter, as she was very special to him. Dressed only in baby doll pajamas, I ran as fast as I could to a neighbour and called the police. In the short time it took me to run next door, he had removed the firing pin from the rifle and hidden it somewhere in the house. When the police came, all they saw was a drunk and a rifle with no firing pin. He must have been convincing when he spoke to them, because they didn't even take him to the drunk tank. I reminded the police that he had hidden the firing pin, but nothing was done. My daughter and I were left with a drunk and a rifle. He eventually passed out.

There was no safe place to run. Women's shelters were not established at the time, and other than the neighbours, I had nowhere to go. My younger brother was my best friend and my only source of strength at this time. He would come whenever I called him to help diffuse a violent situation. His intimidating size would help to settle things down, at least for awhile. My brother told me constantly that I should leave and start a new life so I could find the peace and happiness I deserved.

My brother died in October 1970 in a car accident. He had been drinking and thought he could make it home safely. He was wrong. I was completely devastated by this loss. I never forgot my brother's spirit and still live every day for both of us. Our family buried him on a Wednesday, and on that Friday I picked up my girls and walked out.

We stayed for a couple of days with a friend across the street until I was able to find an apartment and a job. I worked as the caretaker for our building, as the bookkeeper at an auto service centre, and on weekends, as a timer at a stock car racetrack. With these three jobs, I was well on my way to a new life.

I was surprised when my husband attempted suicide after we left. I visited him in the hospital out of basic human decency. I'll never forget the look of hope on his face when he opened his eyes and saw me at his bedside. I told him I was there because he was a human being in trouble, but under no circumstance was I returning. He never stopped professing his love for me.

There is a syndrome that seems to get attached to women who suffer domestic violence. They seem to feel guilty for something they haven't done, as if they deserve the treatment. I never quite felt that way, but my spirit was wounded by his abuse. I believed him when he told me that no other man would ever want me.

He was wrong, of course. I survived, and have moved on to another chapter in my life. I never look back. There are too many tomorrows to live for. I'm truly thankful for my partner in life, and for the many blessings I enjoy in life, and for the opportunities I've been given to work in support of Alberta's children and women.

I firmly believe that, if we are to end the violence against women and children, we must heal the abuser as well as the abused. If we don't, the healing circle will never be complete. Abusers aren't born. They probably start off as bullies at school, and they go on to abuse the women in their lives as adults.

Until that circle of violence is broken, it's important that we all continue to support shelters and other programs that keep women and children safe and secure. Thanks to the support they find at shelters, these women regain the self-esteem and confidence they need to start a new life free of fear and abuse.

I believe that God and the Great Spirit are watching over us. I am a survivor.

> ✠ *Colleen Klein offers this story of her first marriage "in the hope that I will have made a difference if it gives at least one woman the strength to move on." While her role as the wife of Premier Ralph Klein has given her the opportunity to support a variety of worthy causes in Alberta, Colleen devotes most of her time to activities that contribute to the well-being of children and youth. She is a board member and honourary patron of the Awo Taan Native Women's Shelter in Calgary.*

❈ ❈ ❈ ❈

Without Witness

ELIZABETH J.

I am staggered by the brutal and sudden realization that my husband can, and might, kill me. How do I make sense of this new reality? I find myself in mortal danger at the hands of my life partner.

How do I comprehend the conflicting images: romance and danger, love and hate, security and jeopardy, family and enemy, commitment and abandonment? How do I make sense of it? Everything has changed in an instant.

The initial incident leaves no scar or proof. A shock wave spreads through my body, leaving a soul-deep numbing of my spirit. He sees in my eyes that I understand what he is capable of. He smiles at the fear he sees there. He looks enormous, powerful and intimidating. He is a stranger: a Dr. Jekyll and Mr. Hyde.

"What?" he says. "What's wrong now? Don't make a big thing of this!"

I am stunned and silent, confused. His faces changes. He relaxes.

"I'm not angry. Look my pulse is normal, calm even," he says, fingers at his wrist, feeling his pulse. "If I were angry my heart would be racing . . ."

The aftermath is strategic. He minimizes the event, telling me that I've blown everything out of proportion. He refutes my ability to be my own and only witness to this side of his character. The erosion of my sense of reality is insidious. He exaggerates and distorts my behaviour; denies or diminishes his. He is adamant—indignantly injured that I would even imagine him capable of causing harm. He overwhelms me, drowning out my thoughts with his voice. Self doubt creeps in.

A stronger side of me is fully aware of what "almost" happened, recognizes the lethal potential, clearly perceives the threat. I understand that if I do not accept the rewriting of our history I will place myself— and my children—at risk. I am aware at every sensory level that this educated, successful, determined man is capable of murder and there would be no witnesses.

A numb reality sets in where erosion of self, and survival of self, somehow co-exist. A parallel life evolves where we each move in deliberate ways. I am in survival mode, walking on eggshells. He assesses my every move to determine if I pose a risk to his reputation, his reality, his ego. He controls me with a minimum of effort, threatens me through overt and subtle means. He knows my deepest fears and vulnerabilities.

He threatens to take the children away if I leave. He says he'll prove I'm an unfit mother, and I'll never see them again.

"Who would believe you over me?" he scoffs, secure in his authority and reputation. I have become a shadow. Who would believe me? I am very frightened. I must figure out how this happened, but I am so confused. All I do know is that I must protect the children.

He limits my access to money, transportation, communication and recreation. He puts all the bills in my name. My pay cheque barely covers them. He makes work impossible, takes the car, shuts off the alarm, won't get out of the bathroom, hides my purse, interrupts my sleep, throws my dry cleaning in the garbage "by mistake" and won't let me replace the clothes. He leaves in the morning, unexpectedly, without the children and I have to take them to day care. He forgets to pick them up, denies he said he would.

I become his apologist. He drinks more. Criticizes more. He walks into the bedroom, drunk at 2:00 AM, slams on the light and screams at me: "You're pathetic. You're disgusting. Do you know how lucky you are to have married me?" I learn to de-escalate the emotion and remain calm.

The stress builds, and I become ill. I take some time off work. He uses this as proof that I am incompetent. "Nuts," he says. The kids come home from daycare. I give up my job and stay home full-time. I have no income.

He separates me from friends, family and he limits social encounters to those that benefit him. He calls me all day long. Why was the phone busy? Who was I talking to? What did we talk about? He calls a few friends "by accident" to make sure I was talking to them. He "forgets" to give me messages. It is too hard to go out with my friends. On the rare occasions when I do, the children are very upset when I get home and he is seething. I stop going out.

He takes over the grocery shopping. We learn to subsist on macaroni. I make smiley faces on the macaroni in ketchup for the children, stick hot dogs on top for rabbit ears. I ask for more fruit, vegetables and meat. He says I don't make things go far enough, that his mother could make a whole meal from a potato and ground beef. I cash in some beer bottles and buy seeds to plant carrots and peas. He screams that we are not some poor farm family living off the land. He takes over the vegetable garden, and it becomes his hobby. Everything wilts. The peas get fungus.

He entertains clients at restaurants over lunch. He is not hungry when he comes home, and ignores the place I've set for him at the table.

"I'll eat later," he says. He puts a bag of groceries in the fridge, and goes downstairs to drink. He comes up after I've cleaned the kitchen and gets the grocery bag out of the fridge. He pulls out a steak, sour cream, a baker potato and asparagus. He cooks himself a meal, goes to bed at 10:00 PM. I clean up the kitchen again, throw the half-eaten steak into the trash. Can't remember when I last had steak.

He begins to drop in at any time through the day, listens to my phone calls on the extension, reads my journals, laughs at the self-help books I bring home from the library. The become a source for his mockery. I stop going to the library.

I join Al-Anon, and bring home *One Day at a Time*, a book of daily twelve-step inspirational messages. He shoves it—grinds it—into a box of laundry detergent. When I discover it the message is clear. I buy another one, hide it, and make a book cover. Al-Anon lets me bring the children to meetings. They are quiet, and sit playing at my feet. "Keep coming back," the people say, and I do.

Slowly light begins to dawn. I feel less alone. I hear the stories of adult children of alcoholics, and I can see their sadness and grief. In my heart I vow to save my children from this life. I go back to the library. I read everything I can about alcoholism. I scour the self-help books. I read everything about marriage, parenting, communication and anger. I walk into a Cole's bookstore, and a book catches my eye. *Verbal and Emotional Abuse: How to Recognize It and How to Respond,* by Patricia Evans.

Each word is familiar. Each sentence seems to come from my own story. Each paragraph lifts the veil of confusion. Each chapter empowers me. I begin to feel something. The numbness becomes anger. I understand this insidious deceit and that my powerlessness is essential if he is to control me. I have a name for what I am experiencing; it is *abuse* in its many manifestations.

I tell a friend. She believes me. I tell another friend. She also believes me. They stand behind me. I go slowly. I learn quickly. I move forward deliberately. Everything changes on the inside, but on the outside, I use many, many years of survival skills to keep the children and I safe.

He starts to pick on my young son, finding fault with everything he does. It is constant and I cannot always defuse it. My son cries in my arms, and asks me to take him away. I promise my son I will protect him. I tell him he must trust me, and that it will take a little time. He does trust me, and I make a plan.

I successfully deflect and defuse the abuse, and keep the children from harm. I contrive a way to attend a community outreach program through the YWCA Sheriff King Home.

I make an escape plan. I speak to the police to assess my danger. They are concerned and caution me: human beings are unpredictable. I feel frightened. The seriousness of what I am planning is all too clear. I see a lawyer and initiate custody and home possession orders. I am surprised that I can do this. I am surprised, too, that total strangers are willing to help me, that they believe me. I am strengthened by every step towards safety.

Finally, on one unforgettable day, I initiate the detailed plan that will take the children and me to the shelter of Sheriff King Home. It is the beginning of a new life free of abuse.

Three and a half years later we live a peaceful life. Each day is challenging, but within the day are many successes. My children are doing well. We are honest about the past and realistic about the future. We laugh easily today. Life is better than I could ever have imagined. I feel hopeful again.

 *Elizabeth J. is a professional woman who lives in southern Alberta with two teenagers. Her lengthy marriage to an abusive husband ended after she found shelter and counselling for herself and her children. She says she is grateful to the staff at the YWCA Family Violence Centre for assistance in her transition to a new life. Another aspect of her story, "Making Coffee," appears in the chapter called Starting Over.*

⋈ ⋈ ⋈ ⋈

You Aren't Dead—Yet
VICTORIA STEADER

Throughout the long divorce battle, the abuse continued and actually dramatically increased. My ex-husband threatened to kill me, stalked me, tried to make me lose my job, vandalized my rented homes and vehicle, and left horrible and frightening objects around these homes. I had to move on the advice of the police, due to the threats.

To give you an idea about the kind of objects he left, I will give you two examples. Twice he left hypodermic needles filled with something that looked like blood, and a black leather glove with some kind of animal material wrapped around the wedding ring finger, in my mailbox. This was at the time of the O. J. Simpson trial. Once he left some terrible kind of frozen meat in the mailbox. It looked like two hands, severed at the wrists, and covered with dried blood. When I took these to the police station, I was told they were pigs' feet, cut in half, and were often used by people wanting to frighten someone, because of what they looked like.

He terrorized my children and me by telling us repeatedly that the marriage vows were "till death do you part" and I wasn't dead—*yet*. He would tell my children this on visits to him, when I could not comfort them and tell them this was nonsense. He also kept a cross in the matrimonial house I had to leave, and told my children that the cross was to protect the house from me. They were told not to tell me, and I didn't know about this until I went to clean the house after the court finally ordered it sold.

My children had to deal with this despicable lie on their own for almost three years. The fact that I couldn't provide them with comfort sooner still haunts me. . . .

> ✖ *Victoria Steader is the pen name of a woman who lives in central Alberta. "I am a teacher on stress leave due to the actions of my ex-husband," she says. While her difficulties are not entirely behind her, she says her children and grandchildren are "precious gifts from God . . . and a constant source of strength for me." Victoria says she writies to give peace and comfort to other women in a similar situation. "I think this is a wonderful way for women to help each other. I thank you for this idea, and the opportunity you are offering women."*

❈ ❈ ❈ ❈

To Match His Eyes
ARDITH TRUDZIK

"Are you trying to kill me?" Mike was standing in the kitchen, glaring at his green plaid Mackinaw, holding it at arm's length as though it were poisonous.

I was startled. "What's wrong, Mike? I don't understand . . ."

"Green! How stupid can you be? What possessed you to buy green?" Mike shook his jacket under my nose, indignation and anger in his face. It was fall, 1952.

"I thought . . . it would match . . . your eyes."

"But I have to go hunting!" He flung his Mackinaw down. "This coat is dangerous to wear! The other hunters won't see me!"

"Oh, Mike, I didn't think . . ." I twisted in confusion as a sudden wave of nausea sent me retching into the slop bucket. Stooping to rinse my mouth at the hand-basin, I patted my lips with the towel and turned back to Mike.. . . .

The first skiff of snow lay on the fields, smoothing, softening them, brightening the drabness of the countryside. There was an invigorating tang in the air.

"I want to kill a moose." Mike snatched at my towel. His strong hands twisted it so that his knuckles showed white.

I shivered. I could see that he was trying very hard to control his temper, but he was furious. And it was my fault. Oh, why had I bought that green Mackinaw? Matching his eyes seemed such a silly reason. Now those green eyes stared at me with anger. His fingers trembled as he rolled a smoke, taking a long drag, exhaling, glaring at the grey wreath, which dispersed in layers.

"Did you get me a red cap?"

I could only stare with round, frightened eyes. "No," I whispered. "It's green, too."

Mike's mouth twisted, his rage and bitterness almost palpable. "You're stupid! You have to be taught a lesson!" With one yank, he snatched the twisted towel and twirled it around my neck. Tightened it. "Stupid," he raged. "Stupid . . ."

When he saw my eyes glaze, and my breath come in faint gasps, he released the towel and stood back.

I winced while rubbing my swelling neck. Mike cried, "Oh!" He caught me in his arms as I fell to the floor.

"I'm sorry. I didn't mean to hurt you. I just got so mad." He spoke with irritation. "You're alright now, aren't you? Aren't you?" Holding me upright, he gave me a little shake.

"I feel fine," I lied.

✻ *Ardith Trudzik wrote this story as part of a memoir of her marriage.*

At the time, she and her husband lived on a farm in northwestern Alberta, before the installation of rural electrification, running water, and natural gas heating. They spent the first sixty years of their married life on a farm. Now retired and widowed, Ardith lives in Edmonton. She is preparing her stories for publication.

❁ ❁ ❁ ❁

Don't You Cry
DORIS JOHNSON

The little girl shrank down into the middle of the bed where the springs sagged at the lowest point. Maybe the threadbare spread would swallow her.

Don't you cry. The words resonated through every inch of her slight, trembling body. "If you cry, I'll spank you again." Her mother's shadow loomed over her. The new bare bulb could not dispel the pall in the austere room.

She huddled down into the chenille. Her mind darted every which way, trying to flee. She was mesmerized, the command searing her brain and heart like a branding iron. *Don't you cry.* Trapped, she grasped at the shreds of pain, both from her bruised body and her shattered mind, and tried to contain them. But the fragments tumbled into the air like feathers from a broken pillow. She could not speak. Tears blurred her eyes and coursed down white-hot cheeks, but her mouth was silent.

All she had wanted to do was protect her mom and family. If she had admitted where the garish mesh stocking filled with Christmas candy had come from, she would have opened a Pandora's box of verbal and physical abuse upon whomever was in her Dad's path. The girl feared that the mention of the benefactor would stir the delusions in her Dad's mind that often made him accuse his wife of horrible deeds with this man. To say his name out loud was worse than profanity in this house.

The old gent had stopped the schoolgirls and handed each of them a stocking, kindly wishing them a very merry Christmas. Panic had seized the little girl as the dilemma choked her—to flee, or to accept the gift and devise an explanation? Greed, fueled by shortages at home, won out. Once home she furtively rushed into her bedroom and buried the illicit treat under clothes in her dresser drawer. As the days went by, she didn't dare to check if the stocking was still there. Her fear of discovery was like a time bomb waiting to explode.

Bam! Her mother stood before her with the now repulsive stocking in her hand. "Where did *this* come from?"

The girl's fabricated reply seemed plausible enough, but could her Mom tell she was lying? Her mother seemed satisfied with the explanation and the issue rested for a couple of days.

Kaboom! What was Aunt Ethel saying? "Did your kids get one of the stockings filled with Christmas treats from old Andrew? Wasn't that nice of the old fart to treat the kids? Seems to have no family of his own . . ."

Panic in the little girl's mind blurred the rest of the words. She strained to catch her Mom's benign reply, something about, "Oh, so that's where that came from."

Sure enough, the next day, into the back bedroom, the room of reckoning, where the leather strap hung ominously on the wall.

"You realize I have to spank you for lying to me. Why did you lie to me?"

The child's mind tried to form a logical reply. She wanted to explain, "But Mom, I couldn't tell you. Daddy would hurt you again. I lied to protect *you!*" Words tumbled, and became unintelligible.

Tears gushed even before the strap cracked on buttocks. Pain seared through the skinny, little frame. There were more strokes of the strap this time, and the fury seemed more intense.

"Now stop that crying!" Sobs escaped in spite of the little girl's best efforts to suppress them. There was nothing to be done but hunker down into the bed, and will the rough, worn fabric to envelop her. She wished she would never be seen again.

Don't you cry. Then the woman squared her shoulders and set her jaw as she disappeared into the back porch. Sounds of a foreign dialect mingled with the rhythmic hum of the washer. Were the groans from the woman, or from the wringer as it choked on the endless wads of clothing? When she came back inside, her large, strong hands were red and raw from hanging out yet another load of laundry on the frozen clothesline. How she worked to keep this family clean!

> *Doris Johnson was raised in a family of eleven children in a small town in east central Alberta. Married for thirty-eight years, Doris and her husband, Ken, have four grown children and nine grandchildren. She has worked in various clerical jobs over the years, but her chief focus has always been the people surrounding her. In 2005 she struck a new venture, opening a bed and breakfast in her home in Sedgewick, Alberta.*

❈ ❈ ❈ ❈

I Am Cole's Voice
NAOMI JANKE MANUEL

My name is Naomi and I'm the mother of two beautiful children. One boy and one girl. My son is two, born on June 12, 2000. My daughter is under a year old, born on January 17, 2004. I own my own home and I have a great career with a good company.

Some people might read this and think that my life is perfect. If only they knew. If only they looked at the dates more closely. It doesn't add up. My son should be turning four this year, but he isn't, and he never will. My little angel will never celebrate another birthday.

My life changed forever on July 28, 2002. Early that Sunday morning, I was awakened by an assailant pulling my arms behind my body and trying to tape my mouth with duct tape. He then strangled me three times. I was sure I was going to die. During my struggle to get away, I kept asking about my son, who had been sleeping in my room. He told me my son was okay. I wanted to see my child, but he wouldn't let me. I finally escaped to a neighbour's and called police. The assailant was the father of my little boy.

Eventually he was charged with assault, choking to overcome resistance, and forcible confinement. His court date was set for March 2003.

The next four months were spent in and out of family court. I knew this man was unpredictable and dangerous, but because I had no proof to give the court that he was a threat to my son, this violent man was granted visitation. My son's fate was sealed with that horrible decision. On December 2, 2002, my heart was torn out. I received the news that my beautiful, precious angel would not be returning home. My son had been kidnapped and murdered by his father, who then committed suicide.

On December 9, 2002, the day I turned thirty-four, I buried my angel, Cole Evan (Harder) Janke.

I've done a lot of thinking these last few years, reflecting on the past, present, and future. The path I've followed since Cole's death has been long, winding, and very difficult. I often wonder why I'm here, and he isn't. I know I'll never understand, and there will always be questions without any answers, but I do have hope, and I will continue to believe in the sanctity of life.

Every day is a challenge, but I refuse to give in to sorrow because that would mean that Cole's father would win. And there is no way I'm going to let him take my son away from me again. I am Cole's voice. The only way my son lives on is through me. I want Cole to be proud of his mom, as I am so very proud of him. In his two short years, Cole taught me to be in awe of life. Every day is a reason to wake up and discover the beauty that life has in store for us.

Since Cole's death, I've been in a relationship with a wonderful man who has been supportive. He has brought aspects to the relationship I didn't believe existed: respect, trust, and love—three things that should exist in all relationships, but that I had never known. Together we share the love of our baby girl.

Many people have told me how strong and courageous I am. It's ironic because I don't feel strong and courageous. I feel broken and sad. I believe my life will always be bittersweet. Good, bad, happy, and sad, just as most others will live their lives.

I have concluded that I have only two choices. I can either live or not. Although at times life can be very difficult and extremely sad, I choose to live.

Cole, you are part of my soul. I miss you, baby boy!

Naomi Manuel lives in Calgary with her second partner and their baby daughter. She took a leave of absence from her job with Enbridge Pipelines to take grief counselling. "I have been very fortunate, as my company has been very supportive and understanding," she says. "I have friends and family who love and support me. I decided early on that I wanted to celebrate my son's life. I want to share his life story with all who want to listen."

Cruel Lesson

SHEILA BOWKER

I am a humble person with little regard for material wealth. My greatest source of pleasure in life has been involving myself in issues that uphold the working-class right to pride, equality, and justice.

As a part of the working class, I have defied those who attempt to exercise power over others simply because they feel they are superior or dominant. In making my stand, I have been called stubborn, insubordinate, and defiant. It doesn't matter to me. I am strong in my belief that we are all equal as human beings, and no one has the right to demean another. It bothers me that more people don't protect their dignity, and fight against those who degrade them. Sure, it might cost them a marriage and a few empty jobs, but it's better than allowing someone to break your spirit.

My convictions flow from lessons in life.

I moved to Edmonton after I finished high school in Unity, Saskatchewan. I found the big city daunting.

One warm July night in the first year, I encountered a man who would have an intense impact on my life. I was nearing the end of the ten-block walk to my apartment from my job at a convenience store. It was about two in the morning. Why was I walking? I was nineteen years old, and I had no choice. I couldn't afford a car or taxi fare. Then, like now, there is no Edmonton transit service for late-night shift workers. Also, then like now, pretty, young women who walk home from minimum-wage jobs in the wee hours of the morning are perfect prey.

As I approached the corner of the schoolyard, where I could see the lights of my apartment building, a man emerged from the shadows. He asked me if I had seen his dog. I acknowledged him in a cautious manner, kept my distance, and said nothing more than a meek, "No."

I couldn't really see what the stranger looked like except that he was tall, slim, and dark haired. He evoked some compassion in me when he sadly stated that he was taking care of the missing dog for a friend. As I continued to walk past him, I said, "That's awful. I would not want to be in your shoes." The man responded with a sinister, "I wouldn't want to be in your shoes." He hit me on the head with a blow that knocked my 120-pound body to the ground. The force was so great that my shoes flew off my feet. Just like in the cartoons, I saw stars. All at the same time, I screamed a scream I have never heard before or since.

I will always remember the sound of his unfamiliar voice as he dragged me to my shoeless feet and covered my mouth. With a hate-filled voice, he told me to shut up, he had a gun, and he would use it. He continued to hold my mouth with one hand as he marched me, with what felt like a gun in my back, across the schoolyard. That's when we made our first bargain. He said he would take his hand off my mouth if I promised not to scream again. I nodded in enthusiastic agreement, and gasped for life's precious air when he removed his hand.

Believe it or not, I was young and naïve enough that I really didn't know what was going to happen. I whispered to him that I had no money, but he assured me that he didn't want money. He blindfolded me with my sweater, and tied my hands behind my back with his belt. He told me if I would just do what he told me, he would not kill me. There are some things about this encounter that I have never been able to recall all at the same time. My mind only reminds me in bits and pieces of pain and humiliation.

When he was finished sexually assaulting my body, and violating my soul, he removed his belt from my wrists and walked me, still blindfold-ed, to a spot along the fence under a streetlight. He told me to count to one hundred out loud. You know the expression, "I was so scared, I pissed my pants." Well, it's true. While I was counting, I was so scared, I pissed myself. I didn't count all the way to one hundred. I cheated a bit because I heard his footsteps becoming distant, and then I heard a car engine start. I removed my blindfold, put on the clothes that I could find. The breeze was lovely and gentle. The air never smelled fresher. The feel of the grass on my bare feet never felt more real as I ran to the safety of my home.

My life had been spared. Some might say I was fortunate he didn't kill me. However, allowing someone to degrade you in exchange for your life is a bargain of injustice. In those days, sexual assault was called rape. Women who attempted to find justice through the legal system were often further victimized. I knew I would be blamed for being a poor girl who was taking a risk by walking home from work late at night. The fact that I was young and pretty would have worked against me because men are especially attracted to sexually attractive women. It was generally accepted that men were not able to control their sexual urges, and incidents such as mine were the fault of the woman for one reason or another. To attempt to seek justice in court would have brought more shame, not only for me, but for my family also. The only thing for me to do was to suffer in silence.

Dignity is a difficult thing to quantify. I don't know how much was stolen from me that night, but I do know that I felt that even if it had cost me my life, I should have fought my attacker in order to save my dignity. No one gets a chance to go back and change the past, but from that day on, any bargain I made was based on the principle of equality. I learned a valuable lesson from my attacker, albeit he was a vile teacher. I have spent the rest of my life defending my pride with the knowledge that life is not worth living without dignity.

Sheila Bowker died before the publication of Standing Together. *In the letter that accompanied her submission she thanked her partner, John Malthouse, "a true gentleman," for helping her to edit her painful story. A former nursing home attendant and union local president in Grande Prairie, Sheila became an active leader of the Parkdale-Cromdale Community League in Edmonton. The city named a neighbourhood park after her in 2004 to honour her "tireless community work."*

Looking Back
ANONYMOUS

I see a little girl
wearing a dress
hanging below her knees
white socks fallen down
around her ankles.
Black shoes scuffed from wear,
Eyes expressing childhood innocence.

This little girl remembers
a field, she loves the swings,
best of all is climbing the poles.
She is on top of the world.

She remembers car trips
squished in the back with her sisters, playing games
of counting colours of cars
or numbers of Beetle Bugs.

She remembers camping
and eating fresh fish,
fried in butter, oh so good.

She remembers sitting in a hot car,
waiting and waiting.
Becoming cranky, falling
asleep, waking up tired,
hot and sticky.
Father is in there drinking.

She remembers waking up in the night.
Doors slamming, father yelling.
Everyone has to get up,
he has brought home fish and chips.

She remembers the smell of grease
and feels sick and so tired.

She remembers his slurred speech,
his fumbling, his slobbering.
She feels disgust and revulsion
when forced to use his fork.

She remembers huddling under the blankets.
Screaming, the bad words, the sounds of hurting and crying.

She remembers silence at the table.
Eating. No one daring to talk, complain, or leave the plate
with food on it.

She remembers waking up to his weight
The bad smell
rubbing up and down between her legs
and over her stomach.
Heavy breathing, holding her
Tight, tighter. Pushing, pushing her into the bed.
Wetness. Slime. Stickiness.

She remembers silence,
darkness,
waiting,
fear.

She remembers hate,
silent screams,
pain,
loneliness.

She remembers it going in
and out,
Oh, the pain,

Oh please, please stop
It hurts so bad.
Blood, slime, and stickiness.

Over, over, over
Again
Silent nightmare.

She remembers standing quietly
being hit all over
bruises and blood
This time it is her mother,
getting angrier as there is no crying.
Tears are now gone
and will not return.

I see a little girl
wearing a dress
hanging below her knees
white socks fallen down
around her ankles
black shoes scuffed from wear.
Eyes expressing nothing,
They are empty
and staring
sightlessly.

The author of this poem says she hopes her writing will help readers to recognize "the horror and lasting suffering, so they will want to help and be involved with children and women going through this now." After years of childhood sexual abuse, she overcame drug addiction, prostitution, and suicide attempts to become a professional in the field of psychology and family violence in Alberta. Today, she is a happily married with children.

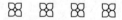

Diary of the Final Month
ANONYMOUS

Halloween 2001
Comes home and screams and swears at me in front of my four-year-old. I start to feel stomach sick, and shake. Continues despite everything in front of my child. Announces he is going on holiday even though he just went on one a few months ago. Says he needs a break. Berates me about my spending. He says: "Don't blow out my brains, or I might get someone to blow out yours . . ."

Nov. 1
"C——. Bitch." He pokes me in the face. "I'll kill you."

He calls the kids and me "savages."

He says: "You never had all this stuff growing up." Grabs me by the neck, and kicks shoe in my stomach.

Nov. 2
Comes home at 9:00 PM. Was in the bar. I am struggling to get my two-year-old to sleep, and ask him to help with the other two. He flies into a rage and bashes a hole in the wall with a hammer. He says, "I could be an axe murderer."

Nov. 3
Hits me on the back of the neck, and threatens to kill me in front of my seven-year-old daughter. My head and neck hurt.

Nov. 4
He pushes me into the fridge, and then against the corner of the breakfast bar in front of my nine-year-old son. Although he had previously said he didn't want supper, he is now screaming at me to get it for him. My son, who is in tears, scrambles to get it for him. He thinks it's my fault because I should have made the supper. Oh my God. Oh my God. Oh my God. He's getting worse. He involves the kids, the poor little kids.

Nov. 5
Right side of my hip is bruised from the corner of the breakfast bar. I take photo.

Nov. 8

"I will bury you."

Nov. 9

"You'll pay in hell." Very aggressive. "Why aren't the kids ready?"

Nov. 10

On phone to his friend, he exclaims: "F——ing kids. I can't stand f——ing kids. . . . They need the leather belt." He kicks my son outside the Hotel Macdonald. There were witnesses, but I was too embarrassed to go and ask for their phone number. Hits me on the back of the neck.

Nov. 12

I'm sorry. Poor, poor kids. I would not have brought you into this for the entire world. Wish I could find a way out for all of us, and some peace. Wish I were stronger, more stable person. Wish I knew what to do. No escape or hope.

Nov. 17

See my husband in totally different light. He is cruel and downright horrible. My youngest won't bathe with him anymore, or let him read her a story. Got to stop looking at big, dismal picture and focus on one day at a time, and the kids' needs. What about my own needs?

Nov. 18

Head-butts me. Calls me a [racist obscenity]. "I know people who I can pay to kill you. I've already talked to one about you." I ask him to lift our two-year-old as I pull out of the driveway. He says: "One less mouth to feed." Refuses. Must protect myself. Must tell myself the pain will go away. All my hopes and dreams are dashed.

Nov. 21

He phones, and asks me to book the Jasper Park Lodge. Puts me in turmoil. I so want to get away.

Nov. 26

He attempts to strangle me, and head-butt me. Thinks I have called 911, and takes off in the Jeep. I can't call, because I don't want to traumatize the children. . . .

This is an excerpt of the author's longer diary. She eventually left her abusive marriage in Alberta to return to her home country. "I think sometimes an abusive relationship just becomes a normal way of life, like living in a war-torn country," she says. "I realize parts of my diary are quite graphic. I wrote it, word for word. . . . I never for a minute regret leaving the hell of what I mistakenly thought was a marriage."

⌗ ⌗ ⌗ ⌗

The Chameleon
FRANGIPANI

I was raped, emotionally, physically, and financially, by my husband—someone I'd invited into my life when I was too blind to recognize the monster within.

The day after we married, I was hurled across the living room full force, face first into a wall. I confided to an older relative, whose reply was: "You married him. You made your bed. Lie in it." Her response planted the notion that my situation didn't warrant repeating.

Initially my mind whirled frantically. What had I done, or not done? Why wasn't I a good enough wife? Why couldn't I make him happy? Love him enough? I was totally stupid, inept. I believed I deserved it. Hell, he convinced me I breathed the wrong way.

If I said hi to a lady, I was a lesbian. Dare I smile at a male, I was a slut. I learned quickly to focus on my feet, not speak unless an answer was demanded. It was prudent to walk out of arm's reach if possible. If I cried, an instant fist connected. He exhibited all the mood swings of a raging, out of control drunk. Ironically we watched WIN House being built. I never suspected my kids and I would seek ten days of refuge there.

Holidays were repetitive living nightmares. Without fail, he would fly into a rage and sweep the meal onto the floor. The second time, I realized this was now part of our life. The rage. The mess. He ran, ransacking the house, cursing everything in his path, desperate to locate "his" marriage certificate. He had to have it—now! Panic city. He pinned me against the wall, spewing, spitting in my face, veins bulging, iron grip. He left me crumpled on the floor and continued his tirade.

He never managed to kill my spirit in its entirety. I eventually retrieved "his" marriage certificate, or ownership papers as he often loudly boasted. I held it above the kitchen sink. Heaven help me, I lit it, and I called him when it was half burnt.

I wore it big time.

I took the kids to the park. My oldest pulled his brother home on the toboggan. I was so sick and exhausted, I fell down. I couldn't get up. "Help!" I crawled the last four blocks home. I was harshly reprimanded for arriving late.

I purposely gained a lot of weight, hoping he wouldn't touch me sexually. I unknowingly made my life nearly unbearable. I was a dirty container. I couldn't wash it away. My mind eventually numbed my body so I never woke up until he was crawling off. The stench made me vomit. My passiveness infuriated him. My fear must have heightened whatever he felt. Soon it became whenever and however he wanted sex. He took it however he could inflict the most pain, mentally and physically. . . .

I'd become a chameleon. In the heat of summer I always wore long sleeves so there would be no questions I couldn't answer. I walked on eggshells forever. He wouldn't speak to me for weeks. Think that's better? Ever heard of anxiety? I was drilled repeatedly, and savagely, that a two-year-old was smarter than I was. That piece of "logic"—and the knowledge that if I died, my kids would be at his mercy, unprotected—started to break the trance. He told me over and over that all he needed to do was beat me over the head with a two-by-four while I slept. He meant it. Nobody would ever know. Who would miss me? No one. Looking into his eyes, where I once thought I saw love, was terrifying. I was afraid to sleep.

WIN House was the destination of our eighth escape attempt. The previous summer, no one would help me. When my address changed to WIN House, opportunities magically appeared. Legal Aid provided a lawyer. I was her first Legal Aid client and she was none too impressed. She might as well have told me to suck it up and get out of her office. She was in no hurry. In fact, she told me I had never asked for custody or a restraining order. I insisted on supervised visitation. It didn't exist. My ex did me the biggest favour ever. He marched into her office, uninvited and unannounced. She called me. Speech wasn't required. His eyes said it all. They scared the hell out of her. Suddenly she couldn't accomplish enough, fast enough. That's when she became my lawyer. I got what I'd asked for, including my final divorce decree. That was the best birthday gift I've ever received, even though I orchestrated it myself.

We moved to a part of the city where I swore I'd never live under any circumstance. Seemed logical. My ex tricked the postal person into showing him the new address. My phone rang day and night. He would pop up all over the place. He even climbed the balcony. I phoned the cops, who advised me to close the drapes in his face. There was only a window between us and his face, mirrored in rage. This was the interlude before the restraining order.

My own sister barely recognized the creature I had become. She told me years later that she didn't think it was realistic to expect me to come back to the family.

An unending, bumpy, rut-filled, winding, scary back road. Twenty years of baby steps. Illuminating lightening bolts. Mental fatigue. Fogged in. Forever exhausted. Focus blurry. Flashbacks. Sleep deprived. Emotionally dehydrated. Grasping at straws. Frustration. Bottoming out. Making decisions. I have clawed my way to life as I know it today, and it is pretty decent! In retrospect, I have experienced ample rewards. I continue to encounter a multitude of hurdles. Life lessons, mostly repetitive. I still have to learn the hard way.

I promised myself I would never be involved with a man again while I had children at home. They would not suffer again because of my bad judgment. I couldn't survive another episode like my marriage. If I couldn't, they absolutely wouldn't. Admittedly I retarded myself socially, but I would keep that promise again in a heartbeat! We moved to a smaller centre. I would walk three blocks out of my way to avoid a male, whether he was fifteen or eighty. Instant panic.

The first casual job I obtained had an all-male population except me. Scary! It was the best thing that could have happened to me. I must have typed my first assignment twenty times—a triple-carbon form, pages long. No mistakes were tolerated. I would think my fingers were poised above the keys, hovering. They shook so badly that suddenly print sped across the page, and I would have sworn I never touched the keys. And yet they kept me.

A baseball bat lay ready under my bed. A cast-iron frying pan decorated my freezer, for unexpected visitors.

I lucked out when I got my permanent job. The trades boys paid me the highest compliment ever. They said I was one of the boys. Y-E-S! But with niceties. I am treated like a lady. I still marvel at all the kindnesses I am afforded daily. I have never been treated so well. They will never know how much they have etched their imprints on my heart. They are very protective. It is like having twenty-five big brothers look out for your best interests. If they take exception to something I say or do, I'm jerked up quickly. If they even smell a situation developing, they run interference and jump to my defence instantly. One of my bosses told me his predecessor warned him to treat me well, or he'd get no co-operation from the boys. That's an exaggeration.

I do know of one guy who refused to do a job because the decision adversely affected me. I pleaded with him to complete it. He would take his lumps. He laid it all on the line for me. Imagine! One of the guys spent a year grabbing me by the shoulders from behind, swinging me around to a smile instead of a fist. He warned me up front; he would teach me that all men weren't pricks. Should someone copy that action unexpectedly, I don't swing at him anymore. I turn ice cold inside, and grow instant goosebumps. I am extremely fortunate in my diverse circle of friends. I would give them the shirt off my back, and they would do the same for me.

I have learned that some hugs actually feel good. Mostly I can say thank you when paid a compliment, and not be embarrassed. I still say I'm sorry all the time, a tough habit to break.

Issues? You bet. I am emotionally incapable of love. Physically? The jury is still out. I wear a ready smile and boast a keen sense of humour—most days. I have finally opened up. I should have done it years ago.

And to you, my friend(s): Initially I was petrified I would say something wrong, afraid that you would vanish as quickly as you appeared. Yet you stayed. Who stood with me always, but especially at my worst? Who empowered me, enabling me to share this crucial phase in my life? You've been there for me whenever I have needed you, asking the tough questions. You have a way of reading between the lines, and drawing out what is really bothering me, even when I don't know. Your patience and understanding—with my torrential tears, when I am unable to speak, you would wait me out. Who lets me get away with nothing, and simultaneously, with everything? You are my personal negativity meter. You defend me to my worst critic—me! Through your gentleness, you made me believe in myself and take risks. What can I say? I will always love you for your unselfish participation in my life.

> ⚜ *Frangipani is the pen name of a woman who lives in a small town in east central Alberta. "I turned fifty this year, and this year is for me," she writes. "Submitting my story is my first accomplishment towards that end. It's a biggie for me." She dedicates this story to everyone at* WIN *House, an Edmonton shelter that she credits for saving her life.*

❈   ❈   ❈   ❈

Empty

KATE DENIS

She sits alone
Her misery spiralling downward
No net to catch her fall
Sick of running
Tired of fighting
Defeated and deflated
She feels nothing
No love, no hate, no joy, no grief
She sinks
Indifference overtakes her
Her soul screams
No way out

She forgets what life was like before
Beaten and broken
She wonders
Will she ever feel again?

> ⚏ *Kate Denis has overcome "a series of toxic relationships, multiple bouts of anorexia, and substance abuse." She has travelled to countries such as Egypt, Mexico, and Malta, returning to Alberta, where she has run her own yoga and motivational speaking business for five years. Kate now works for an Edmonton-based non-profit organization that helps children and teenagers.*

❁　❁　❁　❁

Be Brave and Get Out

ANONYMOUS

I grew up in an era when beating a child was an accepted form of discipline. This beating was sometimes done by hand, but most often with a belt or large clothes brush with worn-down bristles. My dad and stepmother both punished this way, but it was usually my stepmother. She was also verbally abusive. Our friends wouldn't visit at our house because they were afraid of her.

During the time of my childhood, it wasn't normal to run away from home, so all of us children going through this abuse just toughed it out.

A sister who was also on the receiving end of the abuse quit school early and left home to go to work.

I married at eighteen, and left the abuse at home to find out that I'd married an abusive man. He didn't show this side when we dated, but I knew by the time we finished our honeymoon that things weren't going to be very much different than my treatment at home.

I spoke with my minister and explained the problems. He advised me to be patient and give it time.

My husband and I rarely had marital relations except after he had beaten me. I was treated by a doctor for the poundings I took, and I hid from the family when I was bruised.

My dad had died suddenly in an accident at work before I had finished school. My stepmother told me when I got married not to "come running home with your problems," as "you've made your bed, now lie in it." I was told repeatedly by my husband not to tell what was happening, and also not to try running, because he'd track me down and give me worse. In those days there weren't any women's shelters or safe places for women or children to go.

The beatings continued to get worse. He would pin me on my back with my hands and arms trapped by his knees. He'd sit on me so I couldn't move my legs or fight back. I'd learned very early on, however, not to try to fight back, as he hit harder and longer then. Finally, he beat me so badly that the doctor had to come to the house, and this was the last straw.

The next day when he left for work, I swallowed my pride and asked the sister who had left home early if I could stay with her until I got a job, and could take care of myself. I knew I had to get out before he killed me.

I'd worked for about six months, always frightened and worrying that he'd find me. Then it happened. I was working at a bank and when I looked up, there he was. He was very pleasant, and asked if he could come after work so we could talk. I should have known better, but I agreed to meet him. He convinced me that he was sorry, and that he'd never do it again and that he wanted me to come home.

The kind and considerate way of treating me lasted only a couple of months, and then the beatings started again. I was pregnant when it started. He was pleased there was a baby coming, but just didn't control his temper. I was punched and slapped, and I was even pushed down the basement stairs one day.

He would say he was sorry after beating me, and would promise to never do it again. When we were in public, he always put on a real loving show. But when we were alone it was like walking on eggshells, wondering when he'd blow up again.

He'd come home from work in a quiet mood, and wouldn't talk for days on end until one night he'd blow up again, and start hitting. I made the mistake of getting pregnant again, hoping it would make things better. Our life didn't get better. He started staying out later, and sometimes didn't come home. When he did, he was very short-tempered with the children. I worried that he'd start beating on them. I lost a lot of weight and noticed the kids were always more at ease when he wasn't home. I realized that as young as they were, they were being affected by the tension.

One night I was surprised when he said he thought we should get divorced. As sad as I was to see my marriage fall apart, I couldn't help but feel relief that the beatings would end at last.

The judge awarded him visitation rights every second weekend. When the children went for a visit, they came home very upset. It would take a week to get them settled down, and the following week I'd have to talk them into going again. They would cry and ask why I sent them away.

My husband was supposed to pay child support but rarely did. It was very tough trying to raise the children on the very little money I could earn. I took him back to family court over and over to try to get him to pay. He'd put on a good show of "trying to do better" for the judge, but that never went any further than the court. . . .

Finally, in frustration, I told him that if he didn't pay the support, I wouldn't let him have his visits. He threatened to take the kids and not give them back.

He'd drive by the place I lived and sometimes would park across the end of my driveway so I couldn't leave. The harassment was hard on my nerves.

I called the police, who came over and explained to me that until he hurt me again in front of witnesses, they couldn't do anything to help me. I told them about all the years of beatings, and the latest threats, but they just repeated that they couldn't help until he did it again.

I felt so helpless. The court couldn't help me collect the support; the police couldn't help me with the threats of more abuse; I didn't have the support of my family with my emotional or financial situation. Things were pretty hopeless.

I ended up moving away from the area and spent the next several years hiding and looking over my shoulder. I was always afraid.

I really feel that it is a great social improvement that there are now shelters and programs in place to help women and children in abusive and dangerous situations.

Restraining orders and emergency protection orders to keep the abusive partner away don't work unless that partner abides by them. A man who will abuse a woman or child will not stop because of a piece of paper. Abused women and children need the support and counselling of trained people in order to get strong enough to get out of the abusive relationship, and not give into the fear that keeps them there.

We all deserve a life without constant fear.

To everyone who reads my story, I'd like to say: Be brave, and get out of an abusive relationship or home. No matter how many times your spouse or parent promises to stop hurting you, the abuse will only stop briefly until the next time. The abuse will keep getting worse the longer you are in the situation.

Be brave, and get out. You deserve better!

> *The author lives in east-central Alberta. "I own my own home and I have a part-time job in the local library. I'm strong and I'm doing okay. I try to recommend books that will help other people. If my story can help any woman realize there is light at the end of the tunnel, that's what it's all about."*

❁   ❁   ❁   ❁

Abandoned

RACHEL

A young woman sits in a motel room. It is the kind with the off-white cement walls, stained carpeting, dark flowered bedspreads with cigarette holes burned in them. The rain falls, tapping against the windowpane. The rain is so heavy; all images are blurry on the other side of the window. She leaves the dark drapes partially open so she can see the real world pass by in the gloom of the vehicles' headlights.

She sits on the edge of the bed. She looks at her sleeping newborn twins. The oxygen machine drones on and on. She gently adjusts the tiny tube around her son's nose. He stirs and sleeps on in the deep slumber of the newborn. She watches the water stream down the window. She listens to the whoosh of tires hitting the pavement as life passes by her.

She has nothing left. He is gone, and the motel room is not paid for. There is nothing to eat. She has no formula or diapers for her newborn sons. The government worker does not believe her story. The little family of three does not meet the criteria for a women's shelter.

The rain pours down. She cries softly. Finally she succumbs to exhaustion. She curls her body around the babies, and she sleeps a deep sleep. A sleep, for the moment, without the fear of his hands going around her neck, of his fingers closing over her throat. A sleep without the fear of her babies being suffocated, one way or another.

When she wakes up, she is totally alone in a cruel world that has abandoned her with two babies. Her tears fall silently as her two babies sleep on, in the absence of humanity, and in the presence of total darkness and despair.

Rachel grew up in Edmonton, and studied oustide Alberta before returning to the province to teach. Currently, she is raising her children, who have special needs, in Edmonton, and she hopes to return to the teaching profession soon. Rachel says this is only the beginning of her story.

❀ ❀ ❀ ❀

The Stalker
OLGA ROJAS

I was heading nowhere with this man. When I finally came to the decision to call it off, my nightmare began. . . .

He began phoning me incessantly, insulting me, and threatening me. My minister from the Salvation Army advised me to phone the police and file a complaint. That wasn't enough to stop this person. He made it worse for me. He stalked me, broke into my house many times, broke my windows, ripped my clothes, and so on. He would leave messages in my Bible and address book, saying that he was sorry he was doing this to me, that he loved me. I heard one detective say to the other, "This is the worst case of stalking I've ever encountered!"

Once, he was waiting for me at the mall—this happened many times, but in this particular case, when I refused to have a conversation with him, he yelled, "Remember the time you lost your two thousand dollars? It was me who had stolen it from you, you f——ing bitch!" I ran away from him as fast as I could and he followed me in his car. "I am going to make your life miserable," he said. He continued threatening me. I once again notified the police. It was getting worse and worse, to the extent that he even stalked my children and my family. My parents moved in with me. They were scared of what he might do to me. I took him to court twice, but to no avail. On the contrary, he got even madder, totally out of control.

I was forced to move twice, and each time he would find me. Out of fear, I decided to leave my personal belongings at my sister's place. Now, I was certain he was capable of anything. One night, through the bedroom window of my bachelor apartment, he threw a jack that almost hit my daughter or her newborn baby, whom she was breast-feeding. She was so terrified that she moved to Calgary soon after that traumatic and almost tragic episode. My son and I got very depressed. . . .

Fearing the worst, I was contemplating sleeping on the kitchen floor, far from the window, and having the phone right by my side just in case. But I didn't have to. In just a few hours, while I was out, this diabolical human being completely destroyed not only my already scarce furniture and the clothes that I had left, but also the apartment itself, including the medicine cabinet and my precious correspondence material. It looked as if a tornado had hit the apartment.

The detectives came immediately, but were unable to find any prints. It was the "job" of a "professional."

My brother-in-law asked me and my son to move in with them. "He is a coward," he said. "He sees you alone; that is why he stalks you, but I bet that as soon as he knows you are living with us, and that we are protecting you, he won't dare to touch you again." With the little belongings I had left, I reluctantly agreed. I was scared that their home was going to be a target. At night, all occupants of the house would search everywhere, look outside the windows, trying to find or hear something unusual. . . .

Throughout my ordeal, all of my family remained faithfully by my side. . . . I am forever grateful to my parents, my sisters and brothers, and this saviour of mine, my brother-in-law Juan Carlos and his friend Alfredo. . . .

On several occasions, I thought, "When is he going to strike again, or worse? When is he going to kill me?"

I've tried very hard to lead a normal life, and ask God to protect me. Now I am not afraid for my security any longer. Five years have already gone by. Now I think of other victims. I only pray that they would pay attention to certain signs and leave the relationship as soon as possible.

I really wish that no woman would have to suffer like I did.

It wasn't easy for me to recall these incidents. The first day I started writing this story, I couldn't sleep well. However, when I finished it, I felt relieved. Most of all, I know I have been able to overcome the ugliness of that past.

> ⚌ *Olga Rojas immigrated to Canada in 1976. An active member of Edmonton's Chilean-Canadian community, she has been the coordinator of its Literary Contest for three years. She also writes for a Spanish-language local monthly newspaper, Alternativa Latinoamericana, and contributes community notes to the Porto Chileno radio program. "I love doing these jobs as a volunteer," she says. "It is the most rewarding experience for me." Olga is happy to report that she has rebuilt her life after emerging from the abusive relationship she described in this story.*

⊞　⊞　⊞　⊞

Remembrance Day

FAYE LOUISE TESKE

I don't believe there will ever be a single individual upon this earth that will not experience at least a nick to their soul. Having your soul nicked or more deeply stabbed is different than having your heart hurt or broken. . . .

As I reflect back on my life and how early some of those soul stabbings started, and the depth to which they were plunged, I am in awe of how blessed I was not to become bitter and angry at the world. Through God's divine intervention, I remembered joy. I also came to know that the God on the mountain was the same God in the valley. I felt like I was never out of the valley.

When I softly stroke my scars, I liken myself to the elderly war veterans. On our country's Remembrance Day, they stand so proud, straight, determined, pained, with medals polished to a high gleam upon their chests. They witnessed horrors that no one should ever see. They chose not to speak about what they saw, and their prayer is that no one will ever have to go to war again.

I too have seen horrors, lived through slices of time that I want no other person to ever know. When I do speak of those times, it is with the hope that others will understand they are not alone in what they are going through. I pray that as I watch my children grow, they will not be the recipients of my legacy. I have also been blessed with kindred spirits— mostly other women who have received such violent soul stabbings. Some of them bear the physical reminders as well. I have been nurtured by their strength, courage, tears, and faith during times when I felt I just could not endure one more thrust.

As I come to nearly fifty years of life, I look upon myself as fortunate. My life is far, far from perfect or rich, and I am entering a new round of challenges upon my reserves, wondering when there will ever be a time when I will be able to find total calm in my life. When will I know that my time on the mountain has been earned? That I bear enough scars to exempt me for the future? I also hope that day will not come. I live in fear that perhaps I would lose my compassion.

To all of you who read this . . . I hope there will be some resonance within you. Some knowledge that you too have been stabbed. When you meet a kindred spirit, I ask that you offer up a salute and a prayer for her bravery.

> ❖ *Faye Louise Teske, a survivor of an abusive first marriage, found contentment in a third marriage. She says her husband, Doug, is "a man of perception, attuned to my needs, sometimes before I am even aware of them. He provides me with many gifts of the heart: a bouquet of lilacs, creating a flowerbed, being appreciative of small gestures in return. Several times a day, he tells me he loves me. For those women who wonder if there can ever be anyone in their lives, I say, 'Feel the joy of the day. Do not let the harshness and bitterness of the past poison the present. Happiness is there. Before anyone can love you, you must be able to love yourself.'" Faye lives in Leduc, Alberta.*

❖ ❖ ❖ ❖

Out From under the Bridge

TIFFANY

The day was Friday, May 25, and there was a dance at the (northern First Nation) band school. I live not too far away, so I could walk. My cousin Stacey lives with me, and her sister Mandy was here to visit, so we planned on going together with our friends from around here. I think that we all spent at least two hours getting ourselves ready for our so-called "big entrance." Once we were all dressed and prepared for the dance, we walked to the school.

When we got there, we saw a few of our other friends—Sherri, Marcia, and Cynthia. We joined them in having a smoke, and then we headed in. Inside it was dark, except at the DJ table and canteen. We all walked to the middle of the gym, and started dancing and talking at the same time. Alysha, looked down on me, and said, "I admire you for coming here." I just looked at her and asked, "Why?" She said, "Cause of what's been going around about you."

I knew what she was talking about because I had heard the rumours too, but I didn't care. I just felt like hanging out with my friends.

After we got tired of dancing, we took off to my place. Once we got home, we heard there was another party at Jerry's, next door to my house. When we got to Jerry's, I met a guy named Dennis and he kept trying to kiss me, so I just avoided him. Jerry's mom came out and told everyone they had to leave, so we all decided to go to the bridge.

When we got to the bridge, everyone started to talk and get to know each other. I went walking to my friends to talk to them. Suddenly I didn't feel like drinking anymore. I just wanted to be alone. I walked by myself to the other side of the bridge, and went and sat at the edge of the water.

Above me I could hear footsteps, but it didn't occur to me that my friends would be leaving. I decided to look for Stacey and talk to her, but there was no one around. I was surprised that no one noticed that I was not with them. I figured they would come back sometime, so I went to the other side of the bridge where everyone had been. I sat there by myself, throwing rocks in the water, when I heard someone ask if I wanted a beer. I saw Jason walk out from under the bridge, holding a can of beer. I didn't feel like drinking, but I didn't want him to think I was scared to have one beer, so I took it.

After I took a drink of beer, Jason started to kiss me. I was scared because he felt so aggressive. I didn't know what to do, and I didn't want to get hurt, so I let him kiss me. I was trying to crawl backwards, and I ended up under the bridge. Jason lifted me up onto a piece of wood, and pulled down my pants, and forced himself into me. I didn't know what to do, but it hurt so bad, so the first thing I did was slap him. He just kept going, so I pushed him as hard as I could. He fell back, and I pulled up my pants and ran.

As I ran, I started crying. I ran into Stacey, Mandy, Lynette, and Veronica. Stacey asked what was wrong, and I told them what happened. They asked me if I wanted to go home and I said, "Yes." They took me home and put me to bed. When I woke up I was so sore I could barely move or sit down. I looked in the dirty clothes pile and saw that my favourite baby-blue pants had a huge bloodstain on them.

Now, whenever I think of the first time, it hurts. When I tell my friends, they say it was rape, but I never thought so. That must have been because I never thought I would get raped, and I didn't want to say that I was raped. But now, it's not so bad when I think about it, and I can admit that I was raped. It is awkward but I can still get the courage to say I was. I never thought I would lose my virginity to someone I didn't even know, but now I have the knowledge of my experience to share with others.

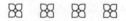 *The author of this story is a Grade 11 student at a school in a First Nations community in northern Alberta. Her English teacher encouraged her to submit her writing to the* Standing Together *project. All names have been changed at the author's request.*

❁ ❁ ❁ ❁

I Take Every Silence and Scream

AMY WILLANS

I will scream no
I will scream it again and again and again
I will not listen to violence
I will fight for my skin
I will fight for my safety . . .

I will fight for my sisters
Yell: KEEP MOVING!
I will take every silence and scream
Every bruise a tear . . .

I will fight for freedom
I won't be afraid to be angry . . .

You will not scare me anymore
You will not steal from me what is not yours
You will not blacken my eye
You will not tell me what I can't say
You will not take, take, take any more

And this is for every woman trapped,
Every woman's sadness
Every woman's fear
This is for voice and clarity
This is for women across borders, in prisons
This is for our blood, our life, our years
This is for our children caught in the middle . . .

And I will scream every word a woman isn't supposed to say
I will scream so loudly it will break doors and windows
I will never, ever be silent again.

>  *Amy Willans is an Edmonton poet. "I intend this poem to be an anthem to encourage women to regain their power. If you've lost it, reclaim it. It belongs to you."*

⌖ ⌖ ⌖ ⌖

Dear Neighbours . . .

BARB M.

I am the person you heard fighting and crying and sometimes screaming. I am the person who lives in the condo, the apartment, or the big fancy house down the block. I am the person you said hi to in the hallway, as you looked the other way so as not to see the bruises. I am the person you saw walking my dog—as you ducked around the corner. I am the person you said hi to in the laundry room. As you left, you said, "Have a nice day!" I am the battered woman in an abusive relationship.

After one of my ordeals, I often sit and cry and wonder how come no one has ever said anything? No one has offered help. No one has mentioned a thing. You are friendly to both me and my partner, knowing what is going on. I wonder if you think at times that I deserve what happens? I wonder if you are afraid to say anything because, after all, I am an adult and I should be able to take care of myself and my problems. I wonder if you think I enjoy the beatings because, after all, I stay and put up with it. The fact is that I have children and a job to worry about. The kids are all in school and are involved in a lot of other activities, so just packing up and moving on, though an alternative, is a very hard thing to do. I am sure the kids would be more traumatized by such a move, and they do love their father. I guess I'm just wondering why you all choose to do nothing or say nothing.

At this point, a smile, a hug, and "I'm here if you need something," would be much appreciated.

The time will come when I am strong enough to leave—when I am finally ready to stand up for myself. In the meantime, a smile from you might just give me that last bit of strength that I need to leave. That short conversation you take the time to make—just by saying, "Are you okay? Do you need something?"—might be just the boost I need. So if you are a neighbour to an abusive situation, take the time and energy to offer a smile, a word or two, or just a friendly face. You don't have to come knocking down my door when it starts, but if I know that you are there, and that you care, it will make a world of difference to me.

It takes a lot of courage to walk away from an abusive relationship, so please don't judge me—just offer a bit of encouragement and acknowledge the situation. And please be willing to listen if I do come to you for advice, or just lend an ear. Talking it out with someone, I might feel like I can do this, and that I am okay.

 *Barb M. says she wrote this story twenty years ago when she was at a low point in her life. She had a twenty-two-year relationship with her abusive partner before his suicide in 1997. "I have been on a healing journey every since," she says. "I have come a long way, but there are so many 'what ifs' and 'I should haves'."*

Barb has six children and fourteen grandchildren, and she is studying full-time to prepare for a new career. "I am thankful that I survived, but I am very sorry that I put my children through so much. If my writing helps just one woman see that she is not alone, and there is help and hope, then I am happy."

⊞ ⊞ ⊞ ⊞

The Tormenting Question

ANGELA LESHER

My story
filled with pain and darkness
will bring disgust to many I'm sure
stop harping on pain, the crowd cries out
what the hell is the matter with her?
why can't she just get over it?
why can't she just let go?
the question of the hour . . . I honestly don't know . . .
the question I scream to myself
over and over.
Just get over it, they say.
For some reason my tires seem to be stuck
in this thick mud, or is it quicksand?

If it is, someone, please don't persecute me.
Take my hand,
I am sinking . . .

 *Angela Lesher lives on an acreage west of Edmonton. She has creat-ed an online support group for women who are emerging from abusive relationships. "My goal is to give the silent a voice," she says. "I somehow found mine after all these years, and I want to help others achieve this same freedom."*

When people ask why abused women don't walk away from violent homes, Angela replies with other questions: "'Why is he hurting her?' 'Why is she being abused?' She is not the one to blame."

⊞   ⊞   ⊞   ⊞

You Begin to Hate Yourself'
VICTORIA STEADER

I am up at 3:00 AM, looking at the stars. I do like looking at the stars, but I do not like why I am up now.

Abuse. I wonder how you can explain it to the people who have never really felt it, lived it, and been it? What surprises me is that abuse is such an "all right" sounding word. It doesn't sound hard, cruel, brash, not like words such as "useless," "bitch," "bad, bad, bad" and other horrible sexual references and vulgarities. That is what the abused people are often called by their abuser. That is what the abused person comes to feel they are.

We study abuse under different categories: physical, mental, and emo-tional abuse. . . . The body, the heart, and the soul know only one kind of abuse. The brain does not separate them into categories and leave us with only the muscle memory of physical abuse, then close down that cat-egory and continue on to a storage compartment to hold mental abuse, and finally send the heart a place to hide and hold the emotional abuse. The abuse is transmitted to every organ, every nerve, every bone, every muscle and every vein of our being. It registers hard and fast and it stays.

Fortunately there are times when it is covered up by some God-given gift of preservation, or what is sometimes called defense mechanisms. But it stays, hard and strong. You have been told: "You are a bad, bad girl. You are a problem. Others have to put up with you. You are lucky to even be here. You are nothing. You don't do anything right. You have always been a problem." This abuse takes hold of your being and it won't let go.

When you are hit, punched, kicked, slapped, thrown around, burnt, left to lie in your own blood, you are sick to your stomach of *you*. You do not hate the one who punched you, made you bleed, called you horrible names. You hate yourself. You know you did something wrong, and that knowledge rests in your bones, in your muscles, in your mind and heart. It becomes you—not a part of you, like a hand or foot, but you. . . .

When the words echo in your ears—useless, selfish child, goddamn bitch, stupid, bad bad girl—your blood turns cold, very cold. It freezes your body and your mind and it tells you to go somewhere else, anywhere else, far away, from the words, the place, and the abuser, away to a nice place, a safe place.

Often this place is a closet or some dark, hidden space. Sometimes it is behind a shed, in a freezing winter blizzard where you wait, pregnant and unloved. Always it is a place where no one can see you, touch you, know you, or hurt you. . . .

Like so many other human conditions, abuse is not curable. It may be alleviated, the pain may grow less intense, but the damage stays. It is as much a part of the person as the air is a part of the atmosphere, as wetness is part of water, as the darkness overtakes even the brightest star.

Victoria Steader is the pen name of a woman who lives in central Alberta. Her first account of her experiences in an abusive relationship appears in the previous chapter. She adds a note of appreciation for the staff at women's shelters across the province: "It was a source of comfort that you were there. I especially appreciated the fact that I could take my children to a place where they would be safe from my ex-husband."

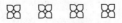

I Can Hear You Calling to Me

TERI RAGO

A mere whisper
A desperate scream

Deep within my soul,
frozen with mistrust,
your voice deflects off this fabricated existence.

And so I turn to the others who can confirm my lie

And so it grows
And I am lost,
but never from my shame

At thirty-one, Terry Rago says she is searching for her own answers through poetry. "Writing has always been a great source of expression for me," she says. "I perceive my collections to be quite dark and raw, but it is in those places that healing does take place. I have been greatly influenced by other women in my life who have overcome adversity, and have given me hope to overcome mine. These women have shown me the importance of needing and supporting one another. My faith in God, and the assistance of other women, gives me strength."

❀ ❀ ❀ ❀

I Didn't Know Anything Else

MITZE WAKEFIELD

Why is it that people need to continue living the same life over and over? I don't really seem to understand how and why we slowly want to return to the abusiveness, as if we need it for some reason.

You know, as a child you don't even realize that everyone doesn't live with abuse. You get older and discover that other people live different lives. That it isn't common to have someone yelling at you, or telling you that you are stupid repeatedly, or that they wished they had drowned you like cats that were not wanted.

I had the crazy idea that everyone wore hand-me-down clothes until high school, and that two sets of clothes is all you have, including your Sunday best. I thought all children, of all ages, helped do chores and field work before and after school, on weekends, holidays, and summer break. Holidays away from the farm? What was that?

My father was mostly physically abusive to himself, driving drunk and smashing every vehicle we owned on the farm. One day the courts decided he should have his licence suspended. He never went back for his licence. He said if they want it so bad, they can have it. Years went by and he would drive or walk or hitchhike to the bar in the small town near our home. He was mentally abusive to his wife and kids right up until he passed away. Funny how he changed when the neighbours or relatives came over. Other people outside the original family never thought the things we said about dad were right.

Sometimes us kids saw Dad holding a knife up to our mother's throat. As you came into the house, asking how to fix something, Dad would turn, holding the knife, saying, "You useless piece of skin, why did I even bother trying to teach you dumb kids anyway?" Mom would calmly ask Dad to put the knife down, and that he was scaring the kids, and he would say, "Who cares?"

I was the youngest of the family. Sometimes I feel I have been chosen to see some of the worst come out of Dad.

I can remember doing chores from as young as six years old. . . . Summer holidays were made up of haying, the old way, tractor pulling the cutter, then the rake, then the baler, and finally the broken-down half-ton hauling the bales home, all loaded by hand.

Chasing a hundred head of cattle down to the well where the water was still pumped by hand was a daily task. Water pumped and carried by five-gallon pails to the pigs and chickens. Feed was bales thrown over a five-foot fence and spread around, and five-gallon pails of chop were carried to the pigs. We did all the things the animals needed: cleaned the stalls out, put fresh bedding down, milked the cows, hauled manure out (when the tractor and stoneboat worked). The milk needed to be separated in the house and then the skim milk fed to the pigs. Time for a little bit of food, fifteen minutes for homework, and then off to bed. As the winter got colder, and at that time calves were born anytime, my father would not call a vet if one was in trouble. When it died, we were told that was our payment for doing the chores all of our lives.

Growing up, I began to understand that other children had chores to do, but not all of them. You make up your mind that when you are done school, you are getting away from this. You want to live a better life. Then this guy comes along who seems to be just right, and lots of fun, so you settle for him. Bang, you're back where you started. . . .

> *Mitze Wakefield grew up on a farm in Saskatchewan, and lived for many years in Lloydminster. She has created a new life for herself and her three teenage children in Chauvin. Her story continues in the chapter called "Starting Over."*

❁ ❁ ❁ ❁

I Stayed Because I Loved Him, Not His Actions
JACQUELINE PIRNAK MARCHAK

I was with my spouse for twenty-one years before I got the courage to leave him. In our marriage, he hit me once. He promised he would never hit me again, and he did not hit me again. However, he began to use a different form of abuse called mental and emotional abuse. I am an optimist; I tend to look at the glass as half full, even when I am down, and believe me, I was down. I started to lose my identity. I did not know who I was, nor did I like what I was becoming.

When someone you love tells you that you're not a good mother, you're not a good wife, you're not good at anything, you start believing it. It's called a self-fulfilling prophecy.

My spouse crippled and paralyzed my children and me with his constant mental and emotional abuse. He would go into rages numerous times a day. It would be over menial things, but we all suffered for it. He would throw things, missing me by millimetres. He would damage property by making holes in walls, breaking furniture, toys, anything in his path. There was continual isolation from family and friends. He would encourage me to go visit, and when I did, he would be upset, so I quit going out. Towards the end of our relationship, I had to visit friends and family, and I didn't care about the consequences because I needed the support. Otherwise I felt things were closing in on me.

He threatened to cut me up and put me in the freezer, and his horrendous verbal comment in front of our three children was: "If you would have had those goddamn f——ing abortions when I f——ing told you to, we wouldn't be having these f——ing problems now." He would call my children "bastard, bitch, asshole, son of a bitch." His famous demeaning name for me was "stupid, f——ing squaw."

So why did I stay for so long? I stayed because I loved him, not his actions. I hoped he would change. My religious belief was that you married for better or for worse. I wanted to make my marriage work, because if it didn't, I would consider myself a failure. I was scared, because how would I provide financially for myself and my three children? I had no job. I previously had left my job because we relocated to northern Alberta for his job transfer, so I was a stay-at-home mom. He did not want me to work, because it was a control issue. He had to have power and control in every aspect of his life, and over those around him. On the day I left, he hit our two-and-a-half-year-old on the thigh, and left marks and welts. His abuse was now directed towards our children in a physical way. That was the turning point for me. . . .

Jacqueline Pirnak Marchak left her marriage on April 16, 1999. "I closed a chapter on my life forever," she says. "It was the hardest thing I have ever done, but it was also the most courageous thing I have ever done." After a brief period in the Hope Haven Women's Shelter with her three children, she resumed her education and eventually received a diploma in social work. Jacqueline now works as a training develop-

ment officer and social worker in northern Alberta. She says she is grateful for the support of the counsellors at Hope Haven, where she found a
new path in her life, and the strength of her faith in God.

"I keep busy with raising three children, my studies, doing volunteer
work, yoga, racquetball, golf, and swimming," she says. "My life is rich
and fulfilling. I think I learned about strength and resilience from my
mother, Sylvia E. Pirnak. I am proud of my Cree ancestry. I am content
and I am healthy in mind, body, and soul. I have control of my life, and
I will not let anyone hurt me again. She adds, "If you are in an abusive
situation, remember you are not alone. Reach out, tell someone, and get
help. Please leave before it is too late."

⌘ ⌘ ⌘ ⌘

It Takes Work

JENNY

It wasn't until I was in the hospital, hooked up to an IV tube, that it
occurred to me. I was sixteen years old, living on my own with a guy, in
what was supposed to be a passionate relationship. We had just moved out
of a tiny basement suite in the inner city to a spacious apartment in the
west end.

I figured things would be better there, but so far, in that week, things
had not improved. They only got worse.

During those days, I had taken a trip in an ambulance for collapsing
and choking on my tongue from anxiety. I had checked into the psychiatric unit, filled out forms for hours, and was given some pills for my
"depression." Those pills were worse than acid. I only tried one, and that
was enough. Then, there I was in the hospital again, with a needle in my
arm that was feeding me sugar because I hardly ate at all during those
stressful days.

I remember having a very brief conversation with a counsellor at the hospital. He asked me a profound question: "Why don't you just leave him?"

I couldn't give an answer. I had never considered leaving him an option. Maybe I never left because I thought people normally got along as we did. It was all I knew or saw. Maybe I had too much pride to go back home or call my family for help. I was almost an adult now; I didn't want to look like I couldn't make it on my own. Maybe I thought this guy was going to get his act together, and take care of me, and we would work things out and get married. I figured things would work out and we would avoid splitting up like my parents divorced. I just wanted to avoid all of the nastiness.

Eventually I did leave.

I asked my grandmother if I could stay with her and her husband for a while. I called my uncle and a friend to help me move my stuff. I can remember my uncle saying, "It's all just stuff—you never see a U-Haul behind a hearse." At the time, neither of my parents could take me in, because they were struggling financially and didn't have any room.

So I started going to school again, and worked a job in the mall. I got my driver's licence and finished my high school diploma, with honours, by correspondence lessons. Gramma took great care of me. I stayed in the rumpus room in the basement, where I spent so much time as a little girl, playing hide-and-seek and toy wars with my cousin.

Every time I came down those stairs to my room, there it was—the spot at the bottom where I had sat on Grandpa's knee. I could remember the smell on his breath from when he spiked his coffee. I could remember the way he touched me down there, and asked, "Do you feel that? How does that feel? Do you like that?" He told me not to tell anybody. When I moved into my Gramma's as an adult, I knew things hadn't been right when I was a child. Moreover, things probably weren't right for Gramma either. That's why they fought like cats and dogs. *That's why he did what he did, and I did what I did.*

Throughout my childhood and youth, my parents were always working. They left me at my Gramma's to stay overnight. I usually hung out with Grampa, though. He exposed me to different kinds of food, like headcheese and oysters. He taught me how to roll cigarettes for him so I could make a little money. He told me to shut the lights off after myself and to be cheap. He showed me his problem-solving and communication skills by screaming, throwing a temper fit, or breaking something. I was pretty used to his style of getting along in life. He had no friends and everybody avoided him. I learned how to avoid confrontation and never spoke up for myself.

After I returned to Gramma's, it didn't take me long to get back on my feet, and out into the real world. I soon discovered that being cheap was sometimes being greedy, and you couldn't attract money to yourself with that kind of mentality. Keeping a secret meant you had to lie all the time, which didn't work in healthy relationships. Throwing a temper tantrum just prevented communication, burned bridges, and closed doors of opportunity.

I have learned a lot from reading books and talking to psychologists, counsellors, friends, and supportive relatives. I practice healthy relation-ships with people, including those I work with. I learn more about the influence of men in my life, day by day, and I have had many boyfriends! Why settle for less than you deserve? Of course, I am not perfect, and I end relationships from time to time, but overall I've learned to take bet-ter care of my needs and myself. I write down my dreams and goals of what I want in my life. I have taken many steps since leaving my ex-boyfriend. I've come to realize that dreams really do come true. Not because of luck, but because of work—hard work. And guts, too.

I am developing more productive and nurturing friendships. I've met many interesting people along the way who have opened doors and given me advice. I've said goodbye to many people along the way, too. I've learned that people come and go in and out of one's life for a reason.

Now, at age twenty-nine, I know myself much more than before. I've found a purpose in life and I am developing a satisfying career. My source—myself, my Creator—has helped me to get here, keeping me focused.

Others have helped me along the way, only because I made the deci-sion to let them. I value other people's experiences, and I belong to a women's success group. We meet in a coffee shop once a week and support each other in fulfilling our goals. We have fun, laughter, and tears, too.

One day at the coffee shop, when I was meeting with this group, there he was—my ex-boyfriend. I tried to hide my face so he wouldn't notice me. Nevertheless, he did, and sat right in front of me with his back towards me. The young girl at the counter knew him, giggled and talked with him for awhile. Then he left. I wanted to warn her about him. She was only sixteen or seventeen, but he was thirty-three now. He hasn't changed a bit, if he still charms the young ones. I felt sorry for her. Also for him.

However, I didn't feel sorry for myself. I could have stayed. I chose freedom instead.

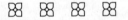 *Jenny lives in Edmonton and works in the financial industry. She says her passion over the years has been volunteerism. She contributes her energy to the Edmonton Non-Profit Housing Corporation, the Edmonton Coalition on Housing and Homelessness, and other organizations. "I hope my story inspires readers to open their hearts, open their minds, and follow their dreams."*

�֎ �֎ ✖ ✖

The Turning Point

Opening the Door

LAURA

Breathe, Laura. Stop this. You've got to breathe! Get a hold of yourself!

I press my back against the moving bathroom door, bracing my feet. He is pounding on the door.

"Open up the door, now," I hear him say, but I am too afraid to comply. "Come on, Laura, open up the f——ing door, now!" He is screaming at me. I look down at the phone clenched in my sweaty hand. Should I call 911? I want to . . . this is so wrong. But what about the repercussions? What am I supposed to do? This is craziness. I can't live like this any longer.

"Laura, let's talk. I love you."

He sounds quieter now, more under control. I walk over to the sink and look into the mirror. I barely recognize my own reflection. Who am I? What have I become?

I am gripping the sink with such ferocity, it scares me. I see my face. It is swollen, mascara-streaked, and puffy from crying. Eyes red and bloodshot.

I am too young to feel like this. I feel ancient. I am tired and worn out. I am not yet thirty. What will life look like for me at forty or fifty? I have no answer, but I do know I cannot do this anymore. It has to end. I cannot see myself at all. Am I lost? Where have I really gone? This is just my shell, trapped and crying in my own bathroom. I must leave him. If I ever get the chance again, I have to take it.

I will no longer believe his excuses, his insincere apologies or rationalizations. It never changes. Never. I've been his partner in this sad, sick dance for ten years. I don't deserve this. I am kind and smart. I am funny and courageous. I will not believe that I am the fat, stupid whore he tells me daily that I am. I need to plan an escape. It will be hard, but it is possible.

"Laura, don't ruin my day. Come on, now."

He coaxes me. I am tempted to open the door as I have so many times.

"You know I don't mean it. Really. You just know how to push my buttons."

Yeah, right. This is not how a healthy relationship works. I am not stupid. I do not make him do anything. I know he makes his own choices. He does have control over his actions. So why am I even considering opening this door? Going into his arms, pretending that everything is going to be fine? No matter how I try, I can't forget or block out the images of our past.

I close my eyes and remember . . .

He is grabbing me by the throat. He pushes me backwards, ramming me into corners and walls until finally he has bent me backwards over the kitchen sink. Oh, God, no. I immediately become still as I feel the sudden cold of the newly sharp blade against my warm throat. My eyes close and time stops. Is this it? I am going to die today. I've finally pushed the wrong button.

"God, Laura, why do you make me do these things to you?" The knife clatters across the kitchen as he releases me.

Time to go numb, and relinquish my care to family and friends. One of them has called 911. The police have arrived and are coming through the back door. They handcuff him and start to lead him away. I see him looking over his shoulder at me. His eyes are pleading with me for rescue. I just watch as they take him, crying as I hold his three-month-old son on my hip.

I wasn't strong enough to end the relationship that time. God, I have become so dependent on him. He has tried to brainwash me to believe I can never make it without him. Yet somewhere deep within me, hope is palpable. My spirit hasn't given up on me, and now it seizes the moment.

I look into the mirror again, and truly see myself for the first time in a long time. I splash cool water on my face. I feel a sense of peace envelop me. I watch the clockwise swirl of the water as it leaves the sink. I am feeling cleansed in body and soul. I have made my decision.

Finally, clarity has replaced fear. I know I need to raise my children in safety, helping them to reach their potential. I want my son to be compassionate, to respect and treat women as equals. My hope for my daughter is that she knows her worth. I pray she grows strong and wise, never tolerating what I tolerated.

I know what I have to do. It's not going to be easy, but I will do it. I promise myself and my children a new life. I open the bathroom door with an awareness of the power of my own spirit. I know I will never be trapped again.

❈ *Laura, a single mother of two children, works full-time in a public school in rural Alberta. "I felt compelled to take a risk by writing and submitting my story," she says. "I saw Ms. Iris Evans on Global TV one morning before work. Usually my routine consists of rushing my children and myself out the door at that time of day. That morning was different. I heard Ms. Evans ask for personal stories from Alberta women. I had a feeling I should take a chance, so I have.*"

Laura says writing this story is the next logical step in her "self-awakening" after her exit from an abusive relationship. "Thank you for giving Alberta women a voice."

※   ※   ※   ※

Buddha's Mercy

YURIKO KITAMURA

night fallen, a darkling fog moving in the house,
    blackout, no light

I know a spider thread holds my life
    it can snap at any time.

in the children's room, time freezes
there is the sweet smell of innocence,
    the peaceful rhythm of breathing,

a beat echoes in midnight air
the night clock ticks, time beats into emptiness
is it my own heart beating?
does time still exist?

I will my hand to clutch the single woven strand

from a deep, dark hole, a fallen soul pulls
    hand over hand,
    on a silken thread
and rises to new life.

Yuriko Igarashi Kitamura is a painter in Edmonton. Born in Hokkaido, Japan, she immigrated to Alberta in 1963 and began her career as an artist. Although she is best known for her technique of dye painting on rice paper, she usually works in watercolours. Her art has been exhibited in North America, Europe, and Asia.

She writes, "One day I was talking to a friend who goes through emotional times. To comfort her, I told her she is not alone, and this is not the end of the world. While I was telling her of my experience, suddenly I heard a voice inside of me saying, 'Did this really happen?' Then I realized that the past was in the distance. Some past memories are frozen, kept inside like ice. Now the ice is starting to melt, changing shapes, becoming less heavy. I still have scars inside. Until now I couldn't write down some of these experiences, but I decided to bring them out. Some day I hope these things, too, will evaporate to air like water."

❈ ❈ ❈ ❈

The Whole Thing Was a Miracle

HANNAH NESHER

I glanced nervously at my watch. A quarter to five. He should be finishing work at five and then be on his way home. "There's no way we're going to get out of here on time," I thought to myself. Once I made the decision to leave, all I wanted to do was get out—quick! I had already contacted the women's shelter, and they were waiting for our arrival. I had a ten-year-old daughter and two babies.

The whole thing was a miracle. When I woke up that morning, I knew I was leaving. I couldn't take the nightmare of the violence in my family any longer. My counsellor said that one day God would give me the strength to leave. That day had come. The problem was that I had no means to leave: no money, no help, not even a cardboard box for moving—just the babies crying on my lap. I sat down and prayed a simple-hearted prayer: *Dear God, if you want me to get out of here, please help me.*

Just then the phone rang and it was a woman from the church, wanting to get together for coffee. I said, "No, but you can come over and help me pack." She brought over the boxes, and we began to pack up my personal belongings. Next came the pastor's mother. She brought a sense of peace and calm to what might have been a chaotic, stressful scene. She held the babies and sang hymns to them while we hurried. She said, "I don't know if what you're doing is right or wrong, but I'm not going to stand by and see a woman being kicked around any longer. I want to help you."

I found a last-minute mover who would take my boxes to a friend's house, but I had no money to pay him. I went to the bank machine and found, to my surprise, that the balance was exactly what I needed for his fee.

As we packed, I kept wondering if I was doing the right thing. My little ones seemed to love their stepfather, but they didn't know that he demanded absolute control and obedience from a woman. Every single detail of my life needed to be cleared past him. Having lived as a single mother for ten years, I was not accustomed to such subjugation of women. Although the pastor and the elders of our church tried to convince him otherwise, he was convinced that his totalitarian dictatorship was all in the name of Christian male headship and female submission. The fact that he had spent time in jail for sexually molesting his adopted daughter, and for assaulting his ex-wife, did not seem to deter him. He was right and everyone else was wrong, in his eyes.

I had quickly learned that it was his way or the highway. This applied to the area of intimacy also. What was meant to be a gift between husband and wife for their mutual pleasure turned into his selfish demands for satisfaction at my expense. Since I often could not accept this, our relationship deteriorated to the point where screaming matches often lasted all through the night. Sometimes I hid in the closet, begging him to leave me alone. I didn't know how it would ever end. I just knew that it was destroying me. Physical pain wracked my body to such an extent that I walked with a limp. And I knew that it was all due to the stress of the strife and violence in my relationship.

I often ran out into the night with my children to try and get away in our van, but he always caught us and dragged us back inside. We lived on an isolated acreage outside the city. Sometimes I was afraid for our safety, but I felt we had nowhere to go. That's when I found out about the women's shelter and went to talk to them. I began to believe there was hope and a way out.

It probably would have ended differently if I had been open and honest with the police or other authorities. When he kicked me to the ground, I just couldn't believe this was happening to me. I wasn't some hooker, some druggie off the street, accustomed to being kicked around. I was an educated, middle-class woman who went to church every Sunday. How I hated to stand next to my husband, and see him lift his hands, singing "Worthy, worthy is the Lamb" when I knew what he was doing to us at home, and how deviously he behaved behind closed doors. My first reaction when I picked myself up off the floor was to call the police. They asked me if he had assaulted me. I hesitated. He was grovelling at my feet, clutching me, crying and pleading with me not to tell the police. Because of his criminal record, he knew they would probably lock him up this time for a long term. Thoughts of being along with the children quickly dashed through my head. How would I raise them alone? How would I support them? What would I do? And so I chose a path of cowardice; I said no. The police asked me again, using a secret signal to let them know if he had hurt me. Again I backed down.

The morning after the physical abuse, I limped into the church service, bruised and broken but still the dutiful wife. A friend who noticed my condition asked me what happened, and I confessed the truth. She was shocked. She began to weep and immediately took me to the pastor's wife. She told me that the church would take care of the situation, and that I didn't need to involve the authorities. How did they take care of it? They simply advised him to stop his sinful behaviour. Not even a slap on the wrist. I felt helpless to change my situation. But I think God heard my cries and saw my weeping. Just as he had compassion on the Israelite slaves in Egypt, so did he have compassion for me. He cares about injustice, and the oppression of the weak and helpless.

At last I decided to leave. As 5:00 PM approached, the mover seemed to be nervous. He said, "I don't want to get involved in a domestic dispute." I didn't blame him. I couldn't predict what my volatile husband would do if he came home to find us fleeing our captivity. So I did what I usually do when I'm in trouble. I prayed again. *Dear God, unless you step in here and intervene in this situation, I'm in big trouble. If you want me to get safely out of this situation, please do something to delay him.* Immediately after this prayer, my husband called to say he had suddenly decided to stay after work for a game of golf. He had never done this before to my knowledge.

I knew God was moving heaven and earth to get me to a place of safety. I found that place at the women's shelter. It has been what seems at times to be an uphill climb to bring my life to a place of healing and restoration, but I will always be grateful that the women's shelter was there for me as a place of refuge. I hope that every woman in an abusive relationship will also find the courage and help to break free, and create a life worth living for herself and her children. As long as there exists that dark place in the heart of man, we will need women's shelters. Thank you. May my story be received as partial payment for an eternal debt of gratitude I owe you.

> *Hannah Nesher grew up in Edmonton and received her Education degree from the University of Alberta. She now lives in Israel, where she continues to write and speak from a Messianic Jewish woman's perspective about current personal and Biblical issues. "I want to encourage women, whether Christian or not, that 'turning the other cheek' doesn't mean we have to live in abusive relationships."*

❀ ❀ ❀ ❀

The Last Day
DAWN HODGINS

I have just turned my last trick. I wait for my mom to come and rescue me from this life that has nearly killed me many times. I have been in this business too long. I am only twenty-three, and I am an eight-year veteran of the street. I am tired, though, and want a new life. I need to be normal, although I am not entirely sure what that means.

I do know that I have not seen 'normal' often in my life. My new friend asked me the other night what I wanted to do with my life. I can't really dream anymore. The only thing I know for sure is I can't do this forever. The violence and drugs will surely kill me. He keeps telling me that I am more than just a sex object. I am not sure that is true, but at this point I am willing to try and find out. My boyfriend hit me last night, and as I stare at the bruises on my chin and neck, I realize these are going to be my last ones.

Am I better than this? Sometimes I wonder. My mom has elation in her voice when I call and say I want to come home. She's here, she's five years sober, and I am ready to be freed from the chains that bind.

We hurriedly pack my stuff—two green garbage bags for ten years of my life—and put it in the trunk of the car. We drive home in silence, mostly, except to stop at McDonalds. I will soon get to see my five-year-old son, and we will finally get to live together.

He runs to me, and gives me a big hug. It feels so good. Then he says, "What happened to you, Mummy? Did Daddy hit you?" So young, but so wise. I tell him the truth, but I also let him know that Mummy won't be getting hurt anymore. It's finally over.

Beginning with that first phone call to her mother, Dawn Hodgins rebuilt her life. Now thirty-four, she lives in Edmonton with her husband, two sons, and three cats. She has worked at the Prostitution Awareness and Action Foundation of Edmonton, and as a research assistant and project co-coordinator for other helping agencies in the city. She attends Grant MacEwan College part-time as a social work student, and she is a passionate public educator, "talking to anyone who will listen about the realities around street prostitution and drugs."

"It feels good to be free," she writes. "I have come to an understanding that maybe I needed to go through what I went through, so I can do what I need to do today. I believe my life has come full circle. And on another quiet Sunday morning, as I sip my coffee and read the paper, I am grateful for love, life, and freedom. Indeed how lucky am I."

❀ ❀ ❀ ❀

Rain on Highway 2

SHERIE VENNER

Rain slid down the windshield, tears of sorrow
I sighed, looking over to my captor, seeing the craggy face
The eyebrows, shading the icy blue eyes of hate
Home, I wanted home, the comfort of the warmth
The arms of my children, hugging me,
squeezing me with their lust for life;
Max, faithful Max, tongue lolling, brown eyes sparkling;
Mom and Dad in the small kitchen, waiting for the phone to sound,
The sounds of pots and pans, the laughs of the babies
Coffee dripping through the percolator

This man changed that,
The wheel turned hard, screeching tires
Signs flashing by, Calgary, 243 KM
Red Deer, coming up
Will he stop here?
I need to call home, tell them I am safe
Am I safe?
No
I don't know what he will do
I am afraid to think of possibilities
I thought he was safe
How could I be so foolish, so trusting?
The red Honda flies above the water
Shimmering across the highway
Fatality signs give futile warnings to the foolhardy traveller
I clutch the side of the grey upholstered door panel
Seeking safety in the touch of the cool fabric

Sssh,
Highway rhythm lulls me, numbs me
Drops of rain creep down my face
He turns, daggers in his eyes,

"Shut up bitch, or I'll shut you up."
Acceleration shakes the frame of the little Honda that could
130 KM per hour
Needle creeping up
140
My life is before my eyes
Snapshots of life with my girls, my reason for living,
They are the valuable legacy of a 17-year marriage

I had been so proud of myself,
Freeing us all from that trap, and leaving safely,
Having him think it was his idea,
When all along I had planned how to get out
Safely

Now another mistake
A big one
How do I get out safely?
Give him what he wants
Let him think it is his idea to let me go
No
I will fight him.
"Let me go now you f——ing bastard! I'll have the cops on you so fast
    your head will spin!"
The car is slowing, crawling now,
Gas station lights up ahead, twinkle off and on.
"Do you kiss your mother with that mouth, bitch?"

What have I done?
"I didn't mean it. I was wrong. I'm sorry, so sorry. It won't happen again.
    You'll never have to see me again. I won't tell anyone. Just take me
    home, please, please."

Calgary
Home of the Stampede
I am quiet now, sunk low, low,

I turn to prayer, to the only God I know
And the meek shall inherit the earth
Maybe
My God is with me in the valley of the shadow of death
I am comforted
I offer up my silent prayer, begging for me,
For the beautiful young daughters I still have to raise.
I promise to become happy with myself
        to not lean on a man anymore
        to define myself,
        to learn how to be enough for me,
        to only invite into my life
        those who can honour me and my children,
        to find boundaries and make them real
        to love myself and my girls enough to learn this lesson
        once and for all, Amen.

The Honda turns into the gas station
A fuel stop at the edge of the universe
Rank fumes fill the air
I sit and wait alone, quiet,
And then the miracle:
Like a horse whose reins have dropped at the end of a long journey
The car turns toward home

"I'll see you around."
"Not if I see you first."
And the chariot is mine again.

Sherie Venner of Edmonton is a mother of five children. Aside from home-schooling her children, she writes in her spare time, and creates theme jewelry and Waldorf dolls.

❈ ❈ ❈ ❈

I Choose Me

TAMARA CHARLES

Growing up, I thought my only choice in life was to live the way mother had lived—on welfare, drinking, addicted to bingo, and being punched and dragged out of bars by a boyfriend who "loved her." She chose the life she led: all of the beatings, the rundown housing, drinking, yelling, swearing, insults, all of it. But that was her choice. My brothers and I grew up surrounded by drug dealers, armed robbers, pimps, anger, fear, beatings, and molestation. We didn't choose it, but that was how we spent our childhood.

One of my clearest childhood memories is hearing my mom cry in fear and pain as her boyfriend beat her. I heard the sounds: my mother being thrown into furniture, beer bottles breaking, threats of what he would do to her, while she begged him to forgive her.

My younger brother and I were hiding in the bedroom when my mom ran in, bleeding and shaking, and gave us a large kitchen knife. She told us to use it to lock the door. Eventually the hitting and screaming and crying stopped and were replaced by muffled groans of a different kind. The next day, she tried to cover up the black eye with make-up, and hid the cuts and bruises with clothes. At six years old, I was expected to go to school and act like nothing had happened. So I did. Covering up the truth became a bad habit that I couldn't break, even when I eventually became the target of his violence.

My mom stayed with this man who beat her. Through another twenty years of black eyes, broken bones, bruises, mental abuse, and even attempting to take her own life, she made us live that same pathetic existence. Welfare cheques went to support beer, cigarette, and bingo habits. Food and clothes were a last priority. He was supposed to be a father figure. My mom took a lot of her frustration out on us, swearing at us, hitting us, and threatening us. When I look back at those events, I know she was using us as her outlet because she couldn't fight back against him. It doesn't make it right. It is just the way it was.

Eventually I took over my mom's role in his eyes.

When I was eleven, my mom became pregnant and he started molesting me. I remember going to school, trying desperately to cover up bruises and hickeys. Teachers just passed it off as if I were "one of those girls." No one ever questioned it. No one asked me if something was wrong. They just assumed I was into boys. I wasn't. I was too scared to tell anyone, so I endured the humiliation because I didn't know better. I figured I was strong enough to get through it until I could leave.

My mom had three boys with this monster, and I became the live-in babysitter while they went drinking or to bingo. Sometimes he stayed home and I felt like it was solely for the purpose of torturing me.

He told me he would teach me how to kiss. He touched me everywhere and told me I smelled like my mother. He told me I liked it. He did everything but rape me. The power he had over me was complete and overwhelming. I was scared of him, and I wanted to kill him. I really did. But I always thought of the consequences, and wondered which was worse: a prison full of criminals, or the prison I was already living in. I chose the five-year sentence of living at home.

When I was fifteen, I was babysitting the boys one day when he came home from work. He was blaming me for not having supper ready, and I said something stupid like, "It's not my responsibility." I knew it would set him off, and it did. He started to punch me, kicking me and throwing me on the ground. He still had his steel-toed boots on, and his physical strength combined with his black rage were enough to cover me in bruises from head to toe. I was so depressed and scared, angry at myself for not fighting back, yet too terrified to run away because I could only imagine what he would do if he caught me. I couldn't stop crying or shaking. I couldn't leave, either. Where was I supposed to go? I had no options—none that I knew about, anyway.

I lived a double life. At school I was a good student and stayed out of trouble. I was a top volleyball player, editor of my school yearbook, on the Grad committee, and I never dated. I knew a lot of people, but no one knew me. I let them think I was this outgoing, fun, charismatic girl who loved life and was on a path to succeed. On the outside I was that girl. Inside I was struggling to stay strong. I was determined not to let him break me.

My saving grace came in the form of a move out of town. The family moved outside the city when I was sixteen and in my senior year of high school. I made the decision to stay and finish school, promising to live with his mother in a retirement home. It was my first step toward freedom, and I took it. At that point I tried to tell my mom what had happened. She shook her head and dismissed it as not being possible. I knew I had done a pretty good job of fooling everyone, including myself, but I could not forgive my mom for choosing him over me.

In 1992 I graduated. I still didn't know how to turn my life around. Instead I became caught up in a romance and I got pregnant at seventeen. There was no choice for me except to have an abortion. I did not want to repeat my mother's experiences. She had me when she was eighteen, and look what happened to her. On my eighteenth birthday I took the bus to the clinic and had an abortion. I don't regret it. I stayed in that relationship for another year, but he broke up with me and I was devastated. Even so, the breakup was the best thing that ever happened to me, because I ended up going to college.

I pursued my dream of becoming a journalist and succeeded. It wasn't an easy success, because I always wanted to go back to the place where I came from. I don't know why. When I met people who worked and paid taxes and were not afraid to go home, I wasn't able to feel completely comfortable in their surroundings. I felt like a fraud, because I came from the inner city, where violence was a way of life. I was afraid to surround myself with people who didn't relate to the life I had gone through. Sometimes I thought it would be so easy to just stay there, and give up. Fortunately I had big dreams. I knew that staying in that environment would slowly kill any hope I had for a chance at peace in my life.

Eventually I had to cut all ties with my family, including my mother and three younger brothers. As there were no guidelines for me to follow, I set my own rules. I looked to my career to fulfil me. It did, and I was on the path to success. While working at a daily newspaper, my path took a sudden turn. I met the man I knew I would marry. He was successful, kind, patient, smart, and funny—I tell him that he's everything I never knew I always wanted. His family life was like something out of that old television series *The Brady Bunch*, yet he never judged me. We have been married since January 2000, and I am finally becoming the person I want to be.

Sometimes an incident will trigger a childhood memory. I will ramble on about being left with babysitters who fed us ketchup sandwiches, or living in houses that were condemned and torn down after we moved out. I try not to think about the really bad stuff, let alone talk about it. I have told only a handful of people about what happened, until now. I have made peace with most of it, and I know that all my experiences shaped the woman I am. Life is a series of choices. I could use my childhood as an excuse to drink and live on welfare with a man who beat me, or I could choose to go for the unknown.

I choose me. I choose to find pleasure in my morning coffee. I choose to find comfort in our calm house. I choose to know that life doesn't have to be a turbulent ride of violence. I choose my husband over my career. I choose my son over myself. I choose a life I never thought would be possible.

Tamara Charles of Edmonton studied journalism at Mount Royal College in Calgary, and worked as a sports writer at various newspapers for almost ten years. Today she works as a communications specialist, writing and designing promotional material for business clients, while she raises her son and awaits the birth of her second child. "I dedicate this story to the thousands of women who think there is no choice. And to my husband, Ron. Without him I don't know if I would have found the strength or courage to tell this story. He has brought laughter, hope, and happiness to my life, and he's been the best choice I have ever made."

The Man Who Wouldn't Leave

MYRNA ERIKSON

He still wouldn't move, yet the house belonged to me. I came home from a staff ball game only to find him on my couch with the boss's young teenage daughter. They had been quite cozy until I arrived. How disgusting of him. Aren't there laws for that? He still wouldn't leave.

Another ball game. I came home to a house full of people. And she was there, too—the minor. I made her leave. Ryan was furious with me. He walked her to her car, and stormed into my house. He threw me hard against the kitchen counter, cutting my hand on a glass when I fell to the floor.

I quickly drove to the hospital and rushed towards a uniformed man. "Are you a police officer?" He told me, "No. Do you need the police?" I said, "I don't know." After briefly speaking to the uniformed man, and the doctor who stitched my hand, I felt there would be an officer waiting for me, and I could get him out. I was half right.

When I got home, an officer had just left. Ryan told the police that I fell, and all of his friends echoed that. Ryan then proceeded to tell me that he told the police that I'd hit him over the head with a baseball bat. The lies!

So the police were not going to help me. I was all alone. I was pretty sure Ryan would hurt my dog if I left, so I couldn't leave her alone. Before falling asleep in a drunken stupor . . . Ryan finished his lickin' on me. He threw me up and against a wooden door. He bashed his skull into my head. He tried to stick his fingers down my throat to stifle my screams. I bit down on those disgusting, nicotine-stained fingers as hard as I could until I saw a scared look cross his face. He got me in a chokehold with his arm around my neck. With his free hand, he pressed my face into the comforter he had bought me the previous Christmas. He only stopped when he no longer heard my screams. I think he got scared that I had actually stopped breathing. Then the little bastard went to sleep, like nothing had happened. It would be a long time before I was ever going to be able to get to sleep again.

My cousin drove me to the police station after that fateful night. The old-world officer paid no never-mind to all the bruising and scratches over my little body. He said: "You should have been there when I got the domestic dispute call." I told him I was in the hospital. That was apparently my problem. Then he stunned me by telling me it would be easier if I left my house until he could get Ryan out. No pictures were taken of my injuries, and a report was filed.

A sheriff was finally able to remove Ryan from my house after two or three unsuccessful attempts. Ryan was now out, but he left me with some major bills to pay. He made a death threat after breaking into my house for the first time. The "visits" eventually ceased.

I now spend time with people who love me. I have taken some more college courses. I have a good job, and a budding career on the way. The man I am in a relationship with now is loving, considerate, and unselfish. I only ever look back to the past as a learning experience.

I survived. Life is good.

Myrna Erikson is the pen name of a woman who lives in west central Alberta. This is an excerpt of her longer memoir of an abusive relationship. She has published articles in several magazines, and she enjoys writing travel and health articles.

⊞　⊞　⊞　⊞

Sleeping Beauty

KATHLEEN YEARWOOD

Last spring I woke up to a whole new world free from abuse. Like Sleeping Beauty, I had been asleep under the influence of a strong poison, and I only woke up after forty-five years. . . .

When I woke up, I was three years into a relationship with a man who was emotionally and physically abusive. He had been physically violent in November, and by March was engaging in an unprecedented level of verbal abuse. Suddenly I saw so clearly what the whole cycle was all about. Something kicked in: a sense of self-preservation and self-worth. I knew—even though it hadn't happened yet—that the next step in the cycle would be a level of physical violence much worse than anything I had ever experienced. I ended the relationship and brought assault and threatening charges when he threatened me. He couldn't believe I had finally put my foot down, and he avoided me.

Our acquaintances and friends, for the most part, coalesced around his denial of the violence, and his description of me as a "bitter ex-girlfriend," but certain people knew the truth and supported me, and those are the kind of people I surround myself with now. Interesting, compassionate, intelligent, and kind people.

I'm no longer fascinated by marginal people with anger problems. I know I needed these people in my life to solve the mystery of why my parents and all the abusive people in my past chose to treat me badly. I know now. It was their choice, and it had nothing to do with me. Beyond that, nothing I could have done would have changed their decision to be abusive.

They are in my past now. I look forward to all the wonderful and happy interactions I will have with my new friends, and by myself, in this newly awakened, beautiful world.

> *Kathleen Yearwood is a composer, a musician, and a novelist. She has published short stories and a novel, and continues to write in a cabin near Vilna, Alberta.*

⊞ ⊞ ⊞ ⊞

Sparks

LESLIE ANN FAHR

In the past, my life has had many seasons, and taken many dark and angry paths. . . .

The real story is about the spark that lay inside me, a spark that I believe is the fire of every woman. It helps women to survive beatings, hate-filled words, and death threats. The spark makes a woman remember her heart, and her fight to live. Sparks are part of the beautiful souls that we all carry.

My spark helped me somehow to complete high school, to get to work most days, and to laugh sometimes. As the years went on, the drugs got harder and I got harder. Yet somewhere a foundation of love lay firm, telling me not to fall too hard, too deep, not to leave just yet.

In my early twenties I began going to college, and in this step began the first spring of my dark life. I was a terrible student, a horrid employee, a terrifying partner, and a lost person. I spent two entire years of college never feeling that I belonged there, and barely making grades. I went anyway, even when I was high or strung out. Why did I do that? Was it the sparks? What really happened was that I began to fight for air and light in my darkness, even though I was still filled with anger, guilt, shame, and drugs. I had begun to let myself feel a little. Some of my girlfriends began to clean up; some even had babies. I began to do work that mattered to me, and I continued to educate myself. I began to care about myself, about living and changing things.

One particular day, something awoke deep inside me that I had never felt before, even as a child. I was at my cousin's wedding—just a wedding, but there was a moment where I saw everything just stop. In that moment I saw who I really was. As I looked around, I saw that they had all loved me all along, and had patiently awaited my return to them from wherever I was. So I returned to my family, facing no questions about my darkness, only an eagerness to know their lost child.

Things have changed rapidly for me since that moment. My connections with my family became strong and beautiful, all of them: siblings, cousins, aunts, uncles, parents, and grandparents. A time came when I decided to commit to life, and to walk away from all the dark places, to start a new life, to be truly me—somewhere safe. . . .

Now I am a professional working with young offenders and women leaving prostitution. I have five years clean with no relapses. It seems that these five years have been longer that the fourteen when I was not really living. Yet I know I still have so much to learn and experience. I still have nighttime dreams of being high, or the old me in my old life. I can actually feel the smoke and the results of inhaling. Only addicts know this painful haunting from the drugs. It hurts. So I am vigilant about who I am now, what my life has become. I know that who I was, is part of who I am.

I am excited about my future—me, the girl who didn't think she would live to see twenty. "Neither did I," said my mother quietly.

I built my life from a garbage heap, and I love it more because of that.

What I do see is that all of us in the garbage heaps of jail, drugs, and hurt are beautiful beings, looking for little sparks to light our way each day. One day they will ignite in an unstoppable fire. I think that the sparks are forgiveness and understanding. Once we begin to allow sparks, we begin to heal and change.

I believe we are all worthy, but we must choose to live or die. Taking my last breath in the darkness of drugs and violence was not a choice I was willing to make. I chose to see, in the sparks, in the darkness. Slowly I built a blazing fire to lead me back to myself.

I tend my fire with vigilance and care, as it is delicate and vulnerable to the harshness of the changing seasons and twisting paths of my journey.

 *Leslie Ann Fahr lives in Edmonton, where she works with young offenders and sex trade workers leaving the streets. "Thank you for this opportunity, mostly a chance to express myself," she writes. "I think this is a great project, and I have forwarded the information to many women I know."*

❁   ❁   ❁   ❁

Reclaiming My Soul
LINDA DUMONT

I stood in the kitchen of the barren, cheap apartment, and felt the emptiness close in. For the first time in more than fifteen years, I was on my own with no one to give me orders. I felt a great loss, as though I had lost myself somewhere, unknown, in those years. I had become a person who no longer existed except in my relationship to others, as a wife and mother. I had value only in my service to others.

During those years I said "yes" to anything and everything my husband wanted, because "no" was far too dangerous. I learned that first year just how dangerous any resistance could be, a lesson that left its trail of scars.

I no longer placed value on my possessions, because anything I had was claimed as his, and he could destroy or dispose of it at will. The home we shared was never mine: the details, even the arrangement of furniture and pictures, and purchasing of groceries, were as he wished. He even chose the clothing I wore: dresses that made me feel like his mother, and nightgowns with so many layers of chiffon that I felt smothered. He insisted I cut my hair, and would have insisted on breast augmentation, too, if we were wealthier.

He watched me constantly and listened to what I said on the phone, or to others, so I spoke little and in guarded sentences. Even so, those carefully chosen words often met with his reproach. "You should have said 'we' cleaned the barn," he said when someone asked me what I had done that day, and I answered, "I cleaned the barn." He had been watching TV, but as his property, what I did, he did—and so it went.

He competed with me endlessly. He had to be the better cook, the better parent, the better person, and the kids and I lied to say he was, although we all knew it was a sham. We secretly shared how we hated the glop he cooked, a concoction of beans mixed with a bunch of other soggy ingredients and cheese. We dutifully ate it. They all agreed that he was a better cook than Mom, because to disagree could spark an outburst of violence. To survive we fostered the lies.

He always hated my paintings. He ridiculed my writing, and made derogatory remarks. He said he was more creative and a better painter than me, although he never even drew a picture. He claimed he was a better writer, and I penned the long, boring, meaningless poetry he dictated because he couldn't even spell.

Looking back, he hated my creativity because it was something that was uniquely mine that he couldn't possess or claim for his own, as much as he would have liked to. He claimed everything else: money I earned, credit for work I did, even my inheritance. I had no will to resist when he insisted on taking my things. After all, to him, they were his. I was his property.

I had learned to do anything and everything necessary to survive. But in that survival, something died. I sensed that there was something intangible missing in myself, but since I didn't know what it was, I couldn't even search for it. There was only that void, a blank, black emptiness that I could push aside when someone needed me. It closed in again when I was alone.

Once he held a loaded gun, and in a drunken fit of remorse, asked me to shoot him. As much as I prayed for his death—"Lord, kill him before he can make it home if he's drunk"—I was afraid to shoot him. Even though I felt that only his death could free me, I was afraid that if I shot him and he didn't die, he would kill us all. That is what stayed my hand, not any feeling of wrongness in killing such a person, or concern for consequences. No prison could be worse than the life I had with him. Even though I dutifully mouthed the words, "I love you," they were as dry and devoid of life as sawdust. I wanted him dead.

He didn't die. And I was running out of time.

I finally left. I met some new friends—through my husband, of course—at a prayer meeting. I never dared to pray aloud, because he would mock my conversation with God when we returned home, emphasizing how stupid I sounded. Despite my guard, I met some new people who had started a street ministry. Suddenly the dreams I cherished as a young woman, before I married into bondage, revived. I felt young and alive, and the dreams were all there.

I could no longer tolerate my prison.

I left with nothing but an old car that burned more oil than gas, my three children, and a laundry basket full of clothing. My street ministry friends took me in until I could find a place to stay, and get on welfare.

Scarred, a shell of a person, I struggled through those first years, trying to make decisions, often making very bad decisions. I relived the past in flashbacks that took me back to the emotions of terror and intense rejection. In the long hours of the night, there were times when I drove the dark streets, weeping hopelessly. I thought of suicide but my children needed me, so I wasn't even free to die. I lived with pain.

Gradually it all came together. I painted, I wrote, and in telling my tale, like the Ancient Mariner, I was healed. After a while I became bored with the tale, and no longer felt compelled to share my past.

The void, that intangible emptiness, became smaller and smaller until one day I realized I was whole.

Linda Dumont lives and works in Edmonton's inner city, where she has edited the Boyle-McCauley News *and published the* Edmonton Street News. *Her reporting, social commentary, and poetry have also appeared in other publications. In 1990 Linda started a volunteer street ministry, Christ Love Ministry. She also paints and teaches yoga classes.*

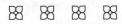

The Breaking Point

ANDREA FIKKERT

You really don't know what you're made of until you're pushed beyond the limit of your endurance. You can guess, but guessing doesn't quite cut it. You hold up or you don't. What quality is it that leaves some women standing in the aftermath of a situation that destroys other women? You might claim it's a matter of will. Maybe it's nothing more that possessing a tenacious, stubborn streak that refuses to lie down and call it quits.

In that split second—head bowed, and on your knees—you break or you don't. You climb back onto your feet and take the next step, or you curl up in the dirt and surrender.

How strong is the woman who has seen herself pushed beyond pride, beyond pain, beyond fear, and has walked away from it a better and more complete person?

I have felt my cheek in the dirt, against the very line of my breaking point, and I cried until my heart broke. I have lived that split second, the moment when there is only one truth remaining. The truth I came away with is that it was not in me to lie down and surrender. When there was nothing left but my faith, and that faith threatened to fail me, I pulled myself to my feet. I took one step, just one. That step led to another, and another. I'm not going to tell you it was pretty to watch, because it wasn't. I didn't stride boldly into the future with my head held high, and all that bull. I crawled. I dragged myself inch by inch to a place where I could once again stand. . . . I can tell you what was in that moment for me. It was an unswerving faith in myself. . . .

What it all boils down to in the end is that I have seen what I am made of. I know who I am. I am that woman who reached her breaking point, and after a good cry, I stood.

 *Andrea Fikkert is a single mother who has seen the darker side of street life and abusive relationships, and has survived them both. She currently owns her own business, and is hoping to find a publisher for a middle-grade children's novel that she and her oldest son have been writing.*

❌ ❌ ❌ ❌

First Time

L. PARKER

It was a time of many firsts

It was the first time my life hadn't gone according to plan
the first time I'd had to live out of a suitcase
the first time I couldn't even use my own name
the first time I hadn't had money to put gas in the car
the first time I'd been on welfare
the first time I'd looked for work because I had to, I really had to
the first time I'd put my kids in daycare
the first time I'd gone to Legal Aid, and then to divorce court

It was the first time I had to convince someone that I wasn't crazy
It was the first time I had known anyone who had committed suicide

It was the first time I'd been a single mom, or a widow
It was the first time I had juggled soccer and utility payments and report
        cards and bath times without any help
First time I realized I could do it without any man
First time I understood that I was wealthy beyond measure
I had my kids, I had my health

At the end of the torrent of firsts
I was able to take my first break from a paying job
I remember getting into my car, and crying all the way home
I was exhausted
I was euphoric
I was so damned proud of myself
I had done it on my own
I was capable of doing it on my own
And I knew it . . . for the first time.

*In this poem, L. Parker describes events that took place twenty years ago.
Married at nineteen to her high-school boyfriend, she became a teacher*

and he became a doctor. He was first diagnosed as a paranoid schizo-phrenic in 1981. In the difficult time before his suicide, Lynn and her chil-dren had to go into hiding in another province. It was a horrific time, she acknowledges, but it ended. "It made me strong. It made me compassion-ate. It made me appreciate what I had. Life is full of surprises."

Today, the author and her second husband live on an acreage near Sherwood Park. They have five children between them, and a grand-child. Lynn works part-time in the family business, tutors students, and enjoys creative writing. She is researching and writing a novel based on her great-grandparents' homesteading experiences. "Life is good."

❋ ❋ ❋ ❋

Seven Boxes

ANNE MARTENS

I knew I had to get away and cut my losses and call it a very expensive learn-ing experience. I had planned to load up my car and drive to Edson. I cried so much, agonizing about what I had to do, that I was sick. I started pack-ing boxes and prepared to leave. He was constantly begging me not to go. My daughter was upset but understood why we had to leave. She's a great, supportive, understanding young lady. She was only a young teen and had already been through more than she deserved.

My car mysteriously started to smoke real bad and ran so rough I could not drive it. I bought that car from my sister and knew it was in good condition—at least, it was until two days before I was ready to leave. Well, his plan to force me to stay was not going to work; I was leaving no matter what. So I loaded about seven boxes, my daughter, and me onto a Greyhound bus. When that bus started backing up, the pain of leaving was so bad and I was so mad and hurt; I hated him so much for doing this to me and my poor innocent daughter. It was a long, very quiet trip to Edson. A long, painful twenty-two hours.

I had a job waiting for me, but I had a very badly sprained ankle, so

I was not sure how I was going to manage. Painkillers work wonders. We had a small one-bedroom apartment with no furniture, except for the seven boxes. They became end tables and dining tables and a coffee table. Walking to and from work was excruciating, but as long as I had my painkillers I was okay. My daughter and I entertained ourselves by playing cards, and going for walks to the library and for picnics in the park. We slowly began to relax and enjoy life. Although she complained of not having a TV, she adapted well. I enjoyed this time, because it gave us time to get to know each other and laugh and play.

As time went on, God again provided for me by sending me the most loving, kind angels. My best friend brought me a box of vegetables from her garden, my cousins brought me a cooler of meat, a co-worker gave me rides to and from work, and friends from my church gave me furniture. It was a good life, and we were free of what's-his-face; bills were slowly getting paid off, although the student loans were and still are a huge burden. We were happy and together and better friends because of it.

Today, after being on my own for quite a number of years and one more bad relationship that I at least had the good sense to get out of quickly, I am in a better place.

I own my own home; I don't have to walk anymore, as I was given a vehicle, and I have paid off all but my student loan bills and the bill I owe my sister for helping me buy my house. My daughter has since moved out on her own, living in Winnipeg, and is doing well. My daughter here in Edson has a great boyfriend and is out on her own and happy. I think playing cards and talking instead of watching TV is a great thing; everyone should try it.

I am in a relationship now with a great guy who is doing so much to help me rebuild myself, and he encourages me to let the past go and to be the best me I can be. He taught me to go forward, and to look out the windshield and not the back window—that the view is much better out of the front window. And do you know what? He is right. I see things so differently now; things are brighter and more positive. I feel stronger and happier.

This wonderful man gives to me and does not take; the only thing he takes is my love, and I give that freely. What I have learned is it's not the end of the world to get knocked down, but it is if you stay down. I went from powerless to powerful, and like the song says, THEY'RE NEVER GONNA KEEP ME DOWN.

P.S. Don't let them keep you down either.

> ✂ *Anne Martens of Edson, Alberta says writing this story helped her get rid of pain and anger about abuse, and helped her to forgive the people who hurt her. "I have gotten on with my life, and I am doing great. I wanted to tell others how they too can make it to the other side and come out stronger."*
>
> *Anne reports "another miracle." She bought the house she has always wanted on a housekeeper's salary, "and all by myself, no co-signer. I was on cloud nine." "I sit and reflect on my life, and I've had some severe setbacks but for some reason I won't let them keep me down. God is my strength."*

❁ ❁ ❁ ❁

The Girl on Route 8

INGE GENEE

We had been living in Lethbridge for less than a year. We could not afford a car yet. We were living in an unpleasant rental duplex. I had no work, and the prospects for something in my area of training were dim at best. I seemed to have come to the end of the road, I had run out of options and I felt that everything was hopeless. I was angry at everything and everyone. I felt like an outsider, estranged from everything, deep in an alienating culture shock. I felt pretty sorry for myself.

The heat of the July day was not making things better. I was sitting in a bus on route #8 in west Lethbridge, on my way to the university through the new subdivisions that were being pumped out of the prairies. My one-year-old son had insisted on sitting in the back, and I had been too tired to object. Now I was fighting an increasingly sick feeling in my stomach. I wondered whether it was bad enough to risk a screaming little boy if I returned with him to the front of the bus.

Across from me sat a very young girl with a baby in a sling and a toddler in a stroller. She patiently played a finger game with the toddler. The baby was sleeping. I was beginning to get used to seeing very young women with multiple children, but this girl was unusually young. She certainly was not older than eighteen.

"Nice day, eh?" she said with a smile.

You must be crazy, I thought, but I said, "Mmm, a bit hot though." And to be polite, I added, "Are you going to the university?"

"Yeah," she said. "I need to change buses there. Do you know how to get downtown?"

"Yes, you change over to the #7 at the university. That takes you downtown."

"How long will it take?"

"About half an hour in all, something like that," I replied. "Have you not been there before?"

"No, I'm new in Lethbridge."

She mentioned a place name in northern Alberta that I had never heard of before, and looked at me with a happy expression on her face.

"I'm so excited," she said. "I'm going to finish my high school diploma, and then I'm going to get my diploma in early childhood education, and then I'm going to get myself a real career. It's a real big city, eh, Lethbridge?"

I had to smile, but it was a wry one at best. What does a person who has lived in Amsterdam for fifteen years say to a person who thinks Lethbridge is a big city? And where did she get this happy outlook, a child herself with two babies, no education, and, I was guessing, no partner?

She told me she was on her way to take the children to daycare so she could register for a high school equivalency program. She clearly thought everything was going her way. How could she be so misguided? What did she think she was going to make of herself? Even if she were to finish high school, and then an early childhood education program, she was looking at best at a life of poverty as a daycare worker, or in some other low-paying job. She had no prospects whatsoever.

Her family was still living in northern Alberta, she told me. She was here entirely alone, except for her children, of course. She looked at them lovingly. So she had no support network, I thought, no one to take the children for an evening when they were sick and she had to work or study. Yet she seemed unfazed.

"So what brought you here?" I asked, bewildered. "Could you not finish high school where you came from?"

She explained that she needed to get away from the children's father. "He has been beating me up ever since we met, and that was not so bad for me, but one day, I realized he was getting close to starting on the kids. I though to myself: Enough. We'll go away, far away, to where he can't find us, and we'll start all over again. That's why we're here." Even her parents didn't know where she was, because she didn't want the young man to know her location.

"We have a great future here," she said. "I feel like we have a fresh beginning." She looked at me with bright and happy eyes. I saw that she meant every word she said. It did not occur to her to feel sorry for herself. Here she was, free at last, to start a new life with her two children. She thought she had just won the jackpot, and she could not believe her luck.

There was something determined about her that made me confident she would succeed. She would work her ass off for a few years in school, get her diploma, and then continue to work her ass off to raise her children. She could not think of anything else to wish for.

This happened five years ago. I find myself thinking of her often. Every time I complain—because my colleagues or students are unpleasant; or I have again not been given a better contract; or I forget to be happy with my partner, who loves me; or with my children, who are happy and healthy and smart; or with my family and friends, who are far away but stay in touch and support me; or with the house and the car that we now do own—I see that girl on the bus. She seemed to have everything going against her, but believed she was the luckiest person in the world, just for getting away from an abusive boyfriend and making a new life for herself and her children. She is one of the bravest people I have ever met.

I never saw her again. I sure hope that boyfriend did not track her down, that her childcare subsidy was not terminated, that she did not fail to finish her high school diploma because her children were sick on the night before exams. Somehow I believe that even if all of that did happen, she would find a way out of her problems to create happiness for herself and her children. When those children grow up, they had better be proud of her. She is a hero if ever I saw one.

> ❖ *Inge Genee was born in the Netherlands, and moved to Alberta with her family in 1997. She teaches linguistics at the University of Lethbridge, and studies Alberta's minority languages. While she still gets homesick, she says she now owns a cowboy hat and believes she has managed to get over the worst of her culture shock.*

❖ ❖ ❖ ❖

I Was Scared and Angry

MORRIGAN

On October 9, 1985, I got on the bus and travelled cross-country with two small children and three suitcases, leaving behind family, friends, a good job, my home, and all my assets. People would tell me how lucky and brave I was. I could not understand how they could think that someone could be brave or lucky if she had to run for her life, starting over with nothing but one suitcase for each of us, not knowing where we would live or when our next meal would be.

My father beat my mom and she stayed. She died after a lengthy battle with cancer when I was sixteen years old. I can vividly taste the pungent odour of fear the first time my husband hit me. I became fully aware of the feelings my mother must have experienced during the beatings I witnessed as a child.

The thing that finally made me want to get out of my marriage was not the beatings I endured at his hands; it was the sexual abuse, not just against me, but other young girls as well. At the time, I never told anyone of the sexual abuse or the sexual behaviours he perpetrated on young girls. I could not bring myself to explain. The police knew about him, and they would come to the house to speak to him. Each time they came, they would look at me as they took him outside, but they never approached me.

I never really knew what was going on, only what he told me afterwards.

One day a detective showed up at the door and asked me to go for coffee. He filled me in on all the details and offered me a solution to the problem, which was to plant evidence against my husband. It was a solution I could not live with at the time, as I was terrified of my husband. I believed the threats he made to me with the loaded gun at his side, telling me that if he could not have me, no one else would. Yes, I believed him.

After the meeting with the detective, I moved out of the house with the children for two months. During that time, my husband constantly stalked and harassed me, and made promises to change if only I would come back. So I did. After a few weeks I realized nothing had changed, or would change. One day, out of desperation, I picked up the phone book and dialed the number to the local shelter. It was because of that call that my children and I found ourselves on the bus on that fateful day in October. I was scared and angry. The man that emotionally, sexually, and physically abused me got to stay in my home, keep his job, and maintain his way of life. Where was my choice?

Morrigan is a pen name. The author was born in Europe, and grew up in a large family. "I was brought up in the generation where women obeyed their men. Unfortunately, the men in my life have been unworthy of that kind of power. Through an abusive father, husband, and common-law partner, I have learned that no person shall ever rule over me again." She now lives in southern Alberta. Another excerpt from her story appears in the final chapter, "Where I Am Now."

❀ ❀ ❀ ❀

Nothing is Impossible

ALVENA LABOUCANE STRASBOURG

In June of 1921, I was born in Owl River, which is located about fourteen miles north of Lac La Biche, Alberta. We moved to Fort McMurray when

I was six months old. My parents were hard-working Métis people, with a strong Christian background.

Fort McMurray was a hamlet of about three hundred people, of which a majority were Aboriginal. When I started school in 1927, I couldn't speak English, because our language spoken at the time was Cree. All the children were the same. I had to drop out of school when I finished Grade 8, because if we had to further our education, we had to move to Edmonton, which no one could afford.

I grew up happy, and we all had to work to help the family. I babysat my little sisters while my mother cleaned house for the bush pilots' wives.

I grew up fast, and by the time I was sixteen, I was married to a man eleven years older than myself. He was a trapper and made good money. My parents thought he was a good man and would make a good living. I really did not want to get married, and I did not know anything about life, not like the children of today. I got pregnant soon after I was married. I was left alone most of the time, because he would go trapping and stay away for weeks. One of my brothers would stay with me, although I had very little to eat, but when my husband came home and sold his furs, we would live well for a while.

Then one day he came home drunk and I did not know what was wrong with him, but my father just happened to come along and told me he was drunk. We had never seen anyone drunk and I did not know anything about alcohol, but I soon learned fast.

After my first son was born, I was moved out to the bush, about thirty miles north of Fort McMurray, never seeing anyone for days or weeks. There I started my days of sorrow and hardship, and by the time I was twenty-four, I had four children.

Being married to an alcoholic is not easy. He would come home and threaten to kill us with his knives and guns. There was nothing I could do, because there was no help like there is today. When I knew he was in the community and he did not get home, I would start to shake because I was terrified. If it were not for the threat with the weapons, I would not have been so scared, because he was a small man and when he was drinking, I could get the best of him. I was there to protect my children and to keep them fed, safe, and warm.

I trapped squirrels and weasels, because I was very handy with a gun. I'd sell my fur to the store for food. I also shot partridges and rabbits to eat.

Once in awhile, he would bring moose meat home, but he did not want any responsibility at all. To keep him in good humour, I would kill myself working, trying to satisfy him when he was home. I had no choice if I wanted to live. There was nowhere to turn and I felt trapped.

Then one day his aunt, who lived about five miles from us, came to visit. She started telling me about the women he was having affairs with. The community was growing, there were more people moving in, but no one lived close to us.

The little shacks we lived in were not the best housing, but I kept them as clean as I could with what I had. I was lucky my children were healthy, except for colds and little illnesses that children get, because there were no doctors. I lived with him for eighteen years. By then, my oldest son was seventeen and working for the Forestry, my oldest daughter was sixteen and going to school in Fort McMurray, and the two youngest, a boy, fourteen, and a girl, twelve, were going to school in Anzac, where we lived.

One night he brought some friends home and they had been drinking from liquor they would order from Fort McMurray.

I had had enough. I got the strength from somewhere and decided to leave, so I packed a suitcase with what I could.

He did not fight back, because his friends were there and he did not want them to know what he was. He was also surprised that I suddenly had the strength to stand up to him. I borrowed five dollars for train fare and went to my mother's in Fort McMurray. I stayed there for two months, and then I made a deal with my brother and his wife to take my two children until school finished in June, and then send them to me. I left and went to Edmonton, where I stayed with my sister.

I was free at last.

After a week I had a job at a dry cleaner for sixty-five cents an hour. It was hard for me at first, because I had no self-esteem and I was very timid and backward. At that time, I vowed to myself I would get to the top, and I think I succeeded. I was living in a little apartment for $12.50 a week in rent. I could not pay too much with the wages I was getting, but at least I was away from the violence and abuse. My parents taught me to work hard and pay for what I wanted, so I never asked anyone for help. . . .

When I think back to the years spent being an abused housewife, I thank God for helping me. I lost my eldest son when he was twenty-four years old. I still have three children and I am a proud grandmother of six children and great grandmother of eighteen children.

Abused women should never give in to their tormenters, because there is so much help and opportunities today, which I did not have when I needed it.

At eighty-four years old, I have a good life and I thank God for my good health. I will keep on helping children, families, and single parents, and maybe I can make someone's life happier.

> *Alvena Laboucane Strasbourg is a Métis elder with a long record of community service in Edmonton and northern Alberta. For many years, she worked as an employment recruiter for Syncrude Canada, and she has served as a board member and volunteer for many other agencies and organizations, including Edmonton's first women's shelter. A longer version of her story is told in her autobiography,* Memories of a Métis Woman.

⊠ ⊠ ⊠ ⊠

Making Coffee

ELIZABETH J.

I didn't believe in body memory until my counsellor suggested that I move the coffee maker to a different spot in my kitchen. I did it to amuse her. The next morning I made coffee facing the doorway. I was very aware of how calm I felt. Curious about this change in feeling, I walked over to the old spot and turned my back to the doorway. The shift in energy was immediate. I realized that this all too familiar position—this location— was about everything that had happened to me through seventeen years of marriage to a brilliant and cruel man who almost destroyed me.

"What are you DOING?" His voice punches me in the back of the head.

"Making coffee," I state the obvious and scoop coffee into the measure, keeping my eyes downcast.

"Spilling coffee, wasting coffee," he corrects me, pressing his finger to the few brown specks scattered on the orange counter, lifting his finger to my face so I can see the 'evidence'.

"Just a few grinds, I'll wipe it up," I say, levelling the coffee scoop, meticulously freeing every loose grind before I bring it out of the can.

"You wouldn't have to wipe it up if you'd be careful."

I stop and turn toward him, resting the scoop on the can rim. "Look, it's early. I'm tired. It's not a big deal, I'll clean it up." My voice is calm, soothing, even. I look at his silk tie, knotted tightly at his throat. I avoid his eyes.

"Not a big deal?" He booms at me. "Not a big deal?" He is incredulous. "Do you know the price of coffee?" He shrieks, "Do you know the price of anything? I work for this coffee, I provide you with coffee. Coffee you drink all day while I'm at work. Coffee you drink for free. Coffee for those stupid, fat schoolgirls you call friends. And you thank me by throwing it all over the counter—that's what you're doing, wasting my money! That's my coffee!!" He is close to my face now, and I feel his spit against my lips.

He grabs my right wrist—the one resting the full coffee scoop on the rim of the coffee can. The coffee scoop flies up, up in the air, and in slow motion it spins, spilling its dark richness onto the white floor, and the full can totters on the counter and tips over. He is in full motion now—my arms wave recklessly about in his grip, coffee spills onto the counter, into the sink, onto the floor, over his polished shoes. He stops then, looks down at the mess.

"Now you've gotten it in my shoes." His voice is soft, quiet, and dripping with anguish. He looks at me and shakes his head. He is deeply hurt that I would have done this to him. He turns abruptly and leaves.

I'm going to puke. But I don't—it's just a body memory, however powerful. Body memory . . . the point is made.

Today the coffee pot is on the counter beside the kitchen entrance. I face the door when I make coffee—and the memories are gone. My neck is no longer stiff when I get up in the morning, and my back isn't as rigid. I'm beginning to relax, or at least I'm not as vigilant. I am learning to recognize the old survival skills that kept me safe, and I'm retraining my mind and body to let go—I don't need to survive anymore, I'm free.

Once, in the early days when I was first separated, I poured a whole scoop of coffee onto the counter and left it there all day. Each time I passed it, I said, "Oops!" It gave me a perverse sense of satisfaction somehow. Now I understand why.

I have come to accept that there are questions to which I will never have answers. I thought that if I contemplated long enough, I would eventually come to understand why he did those things to me. But the reality is that he did them because he chose to. I accept that I will never understand why he chose to. And that's good enough for me to start letting go . . . slowly, but surely.

Elizabeth J. is a professional woman who lives in southern Alberta with two teenagers. Her lengthy marriage to an abusive husband ended after she found shelter and counselling for herself and her children. She says she is grateful to the staff at the YWCA Family Violence Centre for assistance in her transition to a new life. Today she reports that life is better than she could have imagined. "The children are thriving and safe," she says. Elizabeth says that she is retraining herself to be less vigilant, and more able to embrace the fullness of life. "I am hopeful, and finding my way to peace."

Runaway

CATHERINE CARSON

I disappeared with three preschool children, running away from an abusive husband.

It was either that or risk being killed by my husband in a murderous rage, which would have left our three children essentially orphans. He had already made one serious attempt, driving me home before he admitted himself to the psychiatric ward of our local hospital. Instead of stopping at the house, he had continued to the abandoned drive-in theatre at the end of our street. He pulled me out of the car and began kicking me in the stomach and head. My last conscious thought—I was seven months pregnant—was that I must protect my baby by curling into the fetal position. Then he tried to run me over, stopping mere feet from my body. I came to in the car as he was wildly driving to the hospital, crying and begging for forgiveness. Even our marriage counsellor, who had accompanied us, had been unable to help me; she too was assaulted and bruised, although not as seriously hurt as I.

At the hospital, my husband was taken to a locked psychiatric ward while my injuries were assessed in Emergency. The major concern was for the baby. He survived with no apparent ill effects. I had a couple of black eyes and a fractured cheekbone that required surgery. I was left with some permanent nerve damage that still continues to bother me to this day, a slight tingling in my cheek, upper lip, and gums.

The longer we stayed apart, the worse the harassment got. I could no longer drive my car at night, because my husband inevitably appeared on my tail and attempted to force me off the road. The telephone wires to the house I briefly rented were cut twice, until the telephone company ran a set of dummy wires outside and made a secret connection inside. He eventually destroyed our refrigerator after tipping it over twice.

Thanks to my parents' values, I refused to tolerate physical abuse. Emotional abuse was another matter; I didn't recognize it until long afterwards. My parents believed physical violence by either partner was beyond contempt. The first time my husband hit me—a slap that cut my lip slightly—spelled the end of our marriage for me. I vowed he would never get an opportunity to hit me again. I was pregnant, though, and I foolishly believed I could not leave until after the baby was born, and I was back on my feet and self-supporting. The break came before then anyway.

I resisted leaving my hometown, our hometown, for as long as possible. Perhaps too long. I remember arguing with a couple of police detectives who had suggested that I would have to disappear to ensure my safety and that of our children.

"Why should I have to leave?" I asked. "I haven't done anything wrong. Isn't it your job to protect me?"

"Yes, but we would have to put a twenty-four-hour guard on you; we don't have the resources for that."

My escape occurred in the mid-1960s, when there were no shelters for abused women, no support from the police, no support from the community. I remember being told by a psychiatrist that they would not detain my husband in a mental hospital, because he was not a danger to the community, only to me.

"Aren't I a member of the community?" I asked. "No, you're just his wife," was the callous reply.

My disappearance required careful thought and planning. I knew I couldn't arrive in a strange city with no past or job experience and expect to find a good job that would pay enough to support us. I had to have a job before I left. My only skills were in my profession—reporting, a very public profession. I also knew I had to leave my home province of Ontario, because that would be the first place my husband would look for me. I had to move somewhere where I had no family, friends, or contacts.

On Thanksgiving weekend, I wrote letters to major papers across Canada, applying for a job, explaining that I wanted to move and build a new life for myself after separating from my husband, but not going into details. Two days later, my managing editor, in whom I had confided, came out of his office: "I have Andy Snaddon on the phone," Mr. Snaddon was then managing editor of the *Edmonton Journal*. "He wants to offer you a job."

I was to start at the *Journal* in two weeks. Now, I had to plot my actual escape.

I was prepared to walk out of my apartment with the children, with nothing more than the clothes on our backs. I had sufficient funds, plus a loan from my mother to buy what I needed in Toronto and Edmonton.

In the final days before our departure, my husband decided to drive to Vancouver, where his sister's husband had been recently transferred. Each day the children got a postcard from him en route. As the point of no return passed, I swung into high action. I had already had an out-of-town friend book our flight under an assumed name. Now, I arranged for some of my furniture and appliances to be moved to my new home. The rest I sold. A friend would pick it up in his truck and deliver it to my mother's nearby home, where an out-of-town mover would pick it up. My apartment neighbours would be unable to tell my husband much more than that my furniture had been taken away in an old truck. Another friend, again someone whom my husband didn't know, drove us to the airport.

In Edmonton, I quickly discovered that I wasn't alone. A colleague in the same department was in the same position, a single mother of three who had had to leave an abusive husband. The difference was that her husband did not pursue her.

It took many months before I felt truly comfortable in Edmonton. Every time I saw a car like the one my husband drove, I panicked if it followed me more than a block or two, and I took evasive action to see if it continued to follow me.

It took three years for my husband to track me down. I was returning to the office when I noticed him talking to a clerk in the front lobby. I raced upstairs to my editor/friend and told her that I had noticed my husband in the building. She told me to wait in the women's washroom while she alerted the editor, Andy Snaddon. Andy, himself a burly man, met my husband with two other burly senior editors. In Andy's office, my husband said he wanted only to see the children. Andy promised to arrange a meeting in the presence of a neutral third party. He also warned him that if he harassed me in any way, he would have to deal with the power of the paper. The visit, supervised by an off-duty policewoman, went off well. Next day, he took the children shopping and to dinner, then left. Over the years, he would visit periodically, but he never established a close rapport with the boys. My daughter, however, became his advocate, fantasizing that we would eventually get back together. He died relatively young, alone and friendless.

A social worker I consulted after the first visit told me I could run away again, but that my husband would probably find me again. And I would have to keep on running for the rest of my life. Or I could stand my ground and fight. In Edmonton I had the power, thanks to my job and the connections I had made in the community. I chose to stay.

I re-established my life under an assumed name that had no connection with my past. To succeed, I had to discipline myself not to respond to my former name. I succeeded so thoroughly that even now when old friends and family call me by my former name, I find it difficult to respond. I try to explain that person no longer exists. They don't always understand.

Overall, I rebuilt a good life for myself. I had a happy second marriage. I was successful in my career. Unfortunately, my three children inherited their father's manic depression; all three committed suicide. I am raising my teenage granddaughter, and I have good family, friends, and community that enrich my life.

> *Catherine Carson is a career journalist who spent more than thirty years at the* Edmonton Journal *in various editing and reporting roles, before becoming the news editor. Since she retired, she has been working as a freelance writer and editor. "I left an abusive marriage at a time when there was no community support for women who had to run away. Now, of course, help is available to guide you in disappearing; creating a new identity, with documentation to back it up; and providing support in re-establishing yourself, which I think is great." Speaking to women who are experiencing severe violence and abuse, she writes, "Running away is not a sign of illness. It takes strength to leave, as much as to stay in an intolerable situation, however valid your reasons for staying. Remember, sometimes you have to leave to protect your life and your children's lives. Your partner, if determined, will find a way to kill you."*

❁ ❁ ❁ ❁

Facing Goliath

MARINA PHILLIPS

What does courage mean to you? Do you think of the firefighters who lost their lives in the World Trade Center attacks? Do you think of the men and women serving in war-torn countries around the world?

What about the courage to admit a mistake? Or the courage to stop someone from hurting you? Or the courage to stand up for what you believe? Or the courage to just be yourself?

Yes, all those things take courage, but they also have something else in common. Do you think any of those things can be accomplished without feeling some fear? No. There is no courage without fear.

Courage is not the absence of fear, but rather the judgment or decision that something else is more important than the fear. Courage is what you do despite the fear, despite the resistance, despite what you want right now, this minute.

You don't have to show the kind of courage it takes to get on the news. You can show courage every day. It takes courage to go against the words in your head. *That's just the way it is. What can I do about it? I've always been this way.*

For me, courage brings to mind the Bible story of David and Goliath. David had to fight his giant to get into the Promised Land. Don't you think he would rather have been doing something else that day? Fighting a giant wasn't likely at the top of his list. But he chose not to put his current desire over his true desire.

We can all get into our own personal promised land by having the courage to stand up to our own giants too.

It takes courage to end an unhealthy relationship. It takes courage to face the fact that we might need to look in the mirror and change some things about our own outlook that keep us unhappy. It takes courage to fix our lives in a way that is effective and healthy and that will stand the test of time. It's not easy, but it can be done. . . .

Courage is standing up to whatever mental or emotional giant is in your life. Deal with it, and enjoy a new beginning.

This coming year, resolve to live in such a way that courage—not fear—directs your life. Resolve to determine your own worth, not to allow someone else to decide it for you. Resolve to stop working hard to build someone else's dreams. It's time to find the courage to take your future into your own hands and work for what you want.

My wish for everyone is that we find our own personal promised land called the Land of Beginning Again. Where all of our mistakes, our heartaches, our grief and frustrations can just be dropped like a shabby old coat—never to be put on again. And that we have the courage to never, ever look back!

⌗ ⌗ ⌗ ⌗

Never Give Up

KATHY SMITH

I hit bottom when I was ten days from my due date and my husband disappeared for the weekend. That moment is frozen in my mind. Misery and exhaustion coursed through every fibre of my being. I was nine months pregnant, caring for three children in a state of emotional paralysis. Desperate, I found my way to a twelve-step program for families living with alcoholics. Little did I know, it was to change my life. . . .

Our relationship quickly descended into a daily spiral of alcoholism and abuse. He would tell me I was a piece of crap, and I would agree with him. My self-esteem and self-worth were at an all-time low. My home became familiar to the local police force. At one point, I was calling the police three times a week.

One day I woke up and decided I loved myself after all. I had four boys to raise and wondered what I could possibly be teaching them by staying in an abusive relationship. The thought of standing up to the tornado that my husband had become terrified me, but I knew I had to do it.

After enduring fifteen thousand dollars in property damage and spending time in a safe house, I saw my husband charged with four serious charges, including uttering a death threat and criminal harassment.

He was legally removed from our home.

Everything in our lives was totally out of control, including our finances. I soon discovered my home was in foreclosure, I had no access to cash, and, for the first time in my life, I felt the raw panic of not being able to feed my children.

The skills I was learning from the twelve-step program, and the support I was receiving from my sponsor, were the catalysts that turned my life around. I began reaching out for help. I discovered humanity at its finest, just waiting for me. People began helping in droves. I was given cash to pay my bills and food to feed my kids. People who genuinely cared about my family came into my life. The bank and I worked together and I even found a solution to keep my home.

It is a year since my husband was removed from our home. My boys and I are getting on our feet. Within the last twelve months, business opportunities presented themselves in my life that I could only describe as divine intervention. I bid on a prestigious contract and won. I bid on another and another and won.

Today, I have launched my own publication, and I am sustaining my family as a small business owner. I am working day and night, fiercely determined to control my own destiny, financially at least.

My twelve-step program taught me how to release the rage and, most importantly, forgive myself. There's even a part of me that is grateful for my path trodden. I would not be where I am without it.

I still grieve for my marriage, my husband, and my dreams of our fantasy relationship. But I realize that my husband has his own path to tread and his own lessons to learn, as I do. Life is a challenge for me now, but what I've accomplished is rewarding beyond belief. After all, it was only a scant twelve months ago that my life was in a shambles.

What is the most profound lesson I've learned? Never give up on happiness.

 *Kathy Smith works full-time as a self-taught graphic designer and publisher in the Edmonton area. She is the mother of four boys.*

You Are Never Too Old to Start Over

MARY T.

In twenty-seven years of physical and mental abuse, I felt I had no way of escaping the situation, as I felt he would find me and carry out some of his threats. One night he wished out loud at midnight that I was dead. This was the night before my great escape.

On my morning visit to my doctor on December 16, 1986, I was told I couldn't go home any more due to the condition I was in. Terrified, I agreed to go to the Royal Alexandra Hospital's pastoral care lady, who would place me in a very safe place. A place called Hilltop House was agreed upon, even though I was not pregnant and unmarried like the rest of the girls. I was given a new name immediately and became Marg Toby for the rest of my stay there. The doors were kept locked at all times. Only staff were allowed to answer the door when we rang to enter.

To this day, I have kept my papers of all the general rules of the house. I felt safe there, but I had to have so much of my personal items locked up in the office, and even follow curfews like the girls there. . . . If I went out on an overnight pass, all my belongings had to be packed up and stored, because there was no guarantee my bed would be available when I got back. So much for my first Christmas. My two adult children and their families were assured I was safe at last.

Freedom and peace of mind was soon disrupted when the staff informed me a man kept repeatedly calling and yelling to speak to me. The police were called, and his call was put on the speaker phone. I confirmed it was his voice. They informed me that he should be arrested for breaking the restraining order. I informed them of his volatile temper, plus many, many guns with ammunition. I didn't want to endanger them. The police stressed the importance of having absolutely no contact with him and to please get other clothes in case I was being watched.

After many sessions in groups at the house and counselling at the Royal Alex, I felt strong enough to contact a lawyer. The whole process of getting a divorce was very stressful, as my soon-to-be ex-husband tried every trick in the proceedings to block it.

By July 28, 1987, the divorce was final. Once I could hold my head up high and meet people eye to eye, I applied at Lynnwood Extended Care to do volunteer visits with the elderly. I soon found out I had the compassion and sensitivity to work with the elderly. Then I registered at Alberta Vocational College for the Residential Aide Program. I graduated with the top student award, the Edmonton Northlands Achievement Award. By July 1988 I was on staff at Lynnwood as casual and then part-time staff. Wanting full-time work in order to make ends meet, I applied at St. Michael's Extended Care Centre in 1990, . . . first as a nursing attendant. When a chance came up to become a recreation therapy attendant, I gladly accepted, as some staff had language barriers with residents, and I could communicate in Ukrainian.

I have been at the centre for fourteen years. I truly wish to continue until my retirement in March of 2006. All in all, I feel very fortunate to have risen above the years of abuse and control.

I am free to see and visit all of my old and new friends, and best of all, my wonderful two children and their spouses. I now have three grandchildren I deeply love and treasure. I do refuse to date or have any male relationships, and I feel good about that. . . . I still feel very uneasy if I think I might see him with no one around.

> *Mary T. shares a house with a friend in Edmonton. "It's a low-key life, but I love it," she says. "I have my own place, keep to myself, and enjoy my family. I have never been alone with my ex-husband since I left him. To this day I am still afraid of him, but I have made a good life for myself."*

※ ※ ※ ※

The Abuse Had to Stop
ANONYMOUS

I felt like I was reliving my mother's life
Being abused night after night

I was raising my kids how I was raised
All the abuse, fear, and pain . . .

I met someone who wasn't my friend
although I didn't know it then

He was nice to me, gave me anything I wanted
When he had my trust, the beatings started

Beaten with bats, threatened with knives
For the next two years this was my life

Baby number three was on the way
Will she survive? I could only pray

Enough was enough, the abuse had to stop
I picked up the phone and I called the cops

I was part of a cycle I had to break
My kids' futures were at stake

I charged that monster with assault
They slapped his wrists then let him out

The only way I escaped
Was to disappear and hide away

I cut myself off from my friends and my family
To this day nobody can find me

I was a single mother of three
When I went out on my own

I quit drinking and using drugs
I made my kids a home

I gave them the childhood
That I could only pray for at their age

Seeing them safe and happy
Erased all of my pain

Born in the Northwest Territories, the author moved with her parents to Alberta in 1980. She has five children. "I am also engaged to be married to a wonderful man. I thank God every day for the love and happiness in my life." She adds, "My advice to those of you who have walked in my shoes: Make a stand today, and end the abuse."

❈ ❈ ❈ ❈

I Am Never Lonely

MITZE WAKEFIELD

I guess my life changed the day my husband brought home his girlfriend to live with us. Many nights I was upstairs, crying and wondering how I got into this mess. He helped solve some of the stress when he yelled at me one day to "get the hell out and take them damn kids."

Starting over is not easy. You feel bad, lonely, depressed, tired, and scared to death. No one trusts you anymore: the banks, loan agencies, not anyone. You have to get someone to co-sign for any small loan, and big loans are out of the question. Everyone says the bottom has to drop out from under you before you can crawl up again. Sad but true.

So finally, a year later, I landed a job driving a semi truck, hauling bulk cement for Trican. They were really good at giving me a chance to get ahead, and to prove to myself, as well as to them, that I could do this job. I have been there now for two years. My bills are nearly all caught up and the small loans will be paid off in another year. Everything that I have today I will own soon; that is a great feeling.

My family has been helpful with getting me started again, like giving me their old appliances. I can laugh about this sometimes. I would no sooner get an appliance home and it would quit working. So off to the dump I would go, two washers, two dryers, five fridges, and two stoves. All within a year! My oldest sister asked me one time if it would have been easier to rent and have the appliances supplied. I recall telling her, "How would I have so much fun hauling out everyone's garbage if I had only rented?"

My house is an old two-storey that needs lots of tender loving care. I plan to start fixing it up this year. Some people think I'm nuts, and that's okay, because no one is here yelling at me or telling me how or what to do. I'm not lonely anymore either. I have my three small dogs that are always happy to see me when I come home. They lie by me when I'm sick. They look up at me when I'm sad. They never judge and they are always there for me.

Mitze Wakefield loves her job and her new life with her three teenage children in Chauvin. "I also enjoy handwork, scroll sawing, movies, music, and dance," she says. "My housework and yard work are behind, but I will slowly get it done." After her divorce, Mitze took one year of college training and another course to obtain her Class 1 licence as a truck driver. To other women, she says, "Change is hard, but always remember that you are the one who will be glad—no one else!"

❁ ❁ ❁ ❁

I Just Never Felt Sorry for Myself

MARILYN WOLFE

Yes, I was broke, single, and my life had new uncertainties and choices that were not there before. It was okay. Actually, it turned out that this journey had turned into excitement, something that I looked forward to exploring. . . . Soon I learned that the doubts I faced were, in fact, easier than exposing my fragile and priceless life to a man unworthy of my trust.

The focus changed from constantly trying to keep up with his unrealistic demands, and went back into myself. This time my direction transformed me into something better, and stronger, because I had control over my life. I no longer felt like sharing my soul, dreams, and hopes with someone who would criticize me, laugh at me, and tear them apart. I used to feel so embarrassed and stupid for opening up to this type of person, when nothing I did was ever good enough. Looking back, after gaining my self-esteem and dignity back, it is fair to say that he was the one who would never be good enough for the life I wanted, the life I now live.

What possessions could have provided me with the protection I had at the temporary shelter? Nothing! What price did I pay for a warm bed, food, and clothes? Nothing! What was the reward for taking time to reclaim my life and start over? Me!

Who put me in this situation? An abuser.

When I left my husband, I had a ten-month-old girl and a two-year-old little boy with me. I had no money, no friends to stay with, and a body that was gasping from exhaustion. I gave up everything I needed to live, so it seemed. What I really have now is opportunity. Surprisingly, it doesn't matter when or even how the cycle of abuse is stopped. It just matters that it stays stopped. That is never something to feel sorry about!

Marilyn Wolfe is raising her two children in southern Alberta, where she has recently graduated from a business program. "I have a cozy little townhouse, warm furnishings, and art on the walls. My children are healthy and happy, not to mention noisy, demanding, energetic, and well-rounded little folks, so everyone tells me. We are not rich, by any means, but our richness stems from living a life in safety with stability, honesty, and self-expression. Most important, we live in a place where love can grow."

Marilyn says she chose to fight abuse "with my mind. I harvested self-respect and dignity. When I had these, well, there was just no room left for self-pity." She dedicates her story to the Sonshine Centre.

I Made It Through

S.M. HOFFMAN

Our marriage broke down, we split apart, and the kids and I moved on for the second time. We managed to rent a great little townhouse close to my work, my son's bus stop, and the day home my daughter attended. All was well, or so it appeared.

Then the most difficult journey I had yet to travel in my life opened up in front of me. My newly estranged husband cracked. He lost it. He became unstable, reactive, unpredictable, and dangerous. I began to fear for our lives. He threatened me, harassed me, stalked me, and lost complete control of himself, spiralling downward at a terrible rate.

At work I would receive over fifty e-mails a day, telling me what to do with his daughter or how to run my life. He spread vicious allegations about me through our family, friends, and community. He lied to people about me having an affair on him while we were married. He would allege that I lived in the red-light district and called me a "lying, cheating whore," so I often joked in black humour that it was a term of endearment. He called my work dozens of times in a day, picking fights and accusing me of further atrocities. This was all very stressful, but I managed to shelter the children from most of it.

He was not allowed any contact with my son at all for two reasons. He had no rights to him, as I have sole custody, and more importantly, for the abuse he had inflicted. Every chance he got, he would try to make contact. When he was successful, he would attempt to convince my son that I was a bad parent and it was my entire fault that we split up our family. He almost had my son believing that living with him would be better than living with me, or his own natural father! That was the final straw for me.

The police were very reluctant to help me. My situation was not serious enough to warrant any attention. It seemed to me that a cry for help went unanswered, as the only response I received was, "Call your lawyer."

I learned then that you couldn't get a restraining order unless the person actually hurts you. I took measures into my own hands to protect us. I got call display and screened all my calls. I taught my kids to leave answering the phone or door to me. The minute we got home, the doors were locked and the blinds were shut. We were safe in our little fortress. At work I let my co-workers cover for me. I stopped responding to his e-mails and refused to return his calls unless they were directly related to our daughter. I would have a third-party witness at the house every time he was to pick up or drop off our daughter. Finally, I just ignored his existence.

After two long years of fear, battles, lawyers, and obstructions, I made it through. The divorce was finalized with strict boundaries legalized for both parties to follow. I now have very little contact with my second ex-husband. The daycare my daughter attends is our neutral spot for pickups and drop-offs. The routine is currently working. I know the future holds more battles over schools, graduation, and family issues, but for now we deal with the day-to-day things and thank God everyday that we survived the storm.

I am dating again, a wonderful and gentle man who was one of my close circle of friends, the people I leaned on through this hard time. He knows all about both ex-husbands and the events that our family has been through over the last few years. He is one of my very best friends.

My home is filled with love and happiness. My children are healthy, happy, and centred. I am positive and focused on our future as a family. For the first time in my life, I am truly content right down deep into my core being. It feels terrific.

I have forgiven myself for the mistakes I have made in the past. I deal with my daughter's father as minimally as possible, and in time I hope our relationship will mend enough for our daughter's sake. For the most part, I allow myself to be joyful with me and with my kids.

S.M. Hoffman is the pen name of a Red Deer woman.

Freedom

T. M.

I wanted to do more than just survive. I wanted to do more than get through the next day, the next hour, the next minute. I wanted more.

There is so much more to life if we just decide to make a change.

I made a decision. I told myself I deserved a chance. There was a better way to live my life. My child could know what living was all about. . . .

The last night was the worst. Or was it the beginning? I'm still here. Despite the threats, the fear of the gun going off in my ears, the terror of not knowing what to do raging through me, I survived. The police officer said to leave if I feared for my life; the material stuff wasn't worth staying for. My life and my child's future were more important. Then it began: my new life. I bravely stepped out the door, with a suitcase for each of us, and started being honest with myself.

Learning to receive is a gift that developed as we were taken in by family and then friends for months, until we were able to find a safe haven to call home. Home is a private condo with video security and a post office box mailing address. Home is an unlisted number with name blocking and a male voice on the answering machine. For a while, home was a different route, coming and going, just in case we were followed. Home is where we went after our self-defense and tae kwon do classes. Home is lovingly furnished with kind offerings from family and friends. Home is where we are thriving. Home is where we are free.

Our new life is wonderful! It took two years of battling through the legal system, getting past the senseless waste of time and money that occurs when the other party won't mediate. Yes, I am still paying off the legal fees. That was the price for freedom. My freedom has been completely worth the time, effort, and every dime spent!

Peace, happiness, and possibilities now govern our home. My daughter and I made beautiful scrapbooks describing the dreams and goals we wish for our lives. Many wonderful opportunities are presenting themselves to us; we are open to the universe to fulfill our dreams.

We are blessed. I am grateful for the learning that occurred on this journey, in particular the discovery of my true self buried under layers of old beliefs and discarded hopes and dreams, which have been challenged, changed, and embraced. I am grateful for the grace to let go of any resentments and anger towards my ex-partner. I am grateful for the cleansing and power of forgiveness that released his hold on me. I am grateful for learning to stand up for myself, set boundaries, and say no. I am grateful for the hope that has been restored in our lives and the wonderful sense of renewal and joy. I am grateful for the opportunity to rebuild my life in full colour without a façade. I am grateful for learning what kind of partner I really want and know God will provide when the time is right.

My daughter has a true role model now. Her mother no longer settles for the worst in life, but strives for and expects the best, because she deserves it. My new life is created on my terms, propelled forward and guided by dignity, strength, and passion, with every triumphant, glorious step.

> *T. M. is a product manager for a software company in the oil and gas industry. She has travelled around the world, and is an aspiring writer. Right now she says that raising her daughter—"supporting and encouraging her growth, curiosity, and self-awareness"—is her priority. She is currently writing a book for other women who need to leave their abusive relationships in safety.*

Daughters, Sisters, Mothers, and Grandmothers

❈ ❈ ❈ ❈

My Hope Is Named Alyssa

PATRICIA M.

Today I am looking at a beautiful picture of my seven-year-old daughter. She is one of the next seven generations to come, and she will break the downward spiral of abuse in my family.

My mother is a Cree native woman, proud in every way. She now sits handicapped in a wheelchair and incapable of personally making her own decisions. Today I am applying for legal guardianship so she may live and have someone to make decisions for her. My mother gave away her power to my father, who has physically and mentally beaten her throughout the years.

My sister is now a victim to her partner, who has abused her for over ten years. She is living with multiple sclerosis, and incapable of leaving her partner and taking her two children. Her partner beats her every week, and I see her growing weaker with her MS every day.

I grew up and saw my mother in an abusive relationship with my father. At first it taught me how I should live. Later it taught me to teach my daughter to live a different way. For my daughter, I share this story so other women can overcome the difficulties of abuse.

I saw the countless arguments, as I stood shaking and crying in the corner of the family room, watching my father hit my mother. One day I knew I must do something. I was in my bedroom downstairs, overhearing another argument. Then I heard my mother fall with a thud to the floor. I ran upstairs to see my sister and brother yelling at my father to stop as he stomped and kicked my mother. Then I heard the sound of bones breaking and cracking as I saw my father stomping on her hip. I ran to the phone to call for help, but my father started to chase me and the phone came ripping out of the wall. I then ran into the kitchen, behind my mother on the floor, and yelled at my father: "Step away from her NOW!" He stood there, looking at me, and realized what he was doing and walked away. My sister and brother were standing behind me, screaming and crying for someone to help and hold them. It was here I knew I needed to watch over my family. It wasn't the last time my father physically abused my sister and brother or me.

I met my first boyfriend when I was nineteen years old. Wayne was the world to me. His possessiveness must have meant that he loved me. I had never known my father to even say, "I love you" to me. I thought for sure that Wayne loved me. I stayed home to bake, cook, and do his laundry for him. I must have been a bad cook, because he threw his supper on the floor and told me how bad a cook I was. I will try better next time, I thought. He would walk me to the bus stop, just to make sure no man would pick me up. I would dress nice for him. I could not dress this way without Wayne around, as he would tear all my dresses and mark my shoes with his felt pen. I was walking out the door one day to go to work, when he asked me why I was leaving dressed like a whore. I stood there quietly, not knowing what to say, as I didn't want to upset him. He proceeded to knock me to the ground and rip my skirt off without taking my shoes off. This was his way of making sure I walked out the door, dressed the way he wanted.

I knew in my heart something was wrong. I started to go to counselling and learned I had rights. I bought a book called *Women Who Love Too Much*, the book that saved my life. Wayne started to see the change in me, and was getting suspicious. He found my book and threw it out. Wayne had a horrific and volatile temper. One day I came home to find all of my possessions lying on the front lawn because I was late coming home from work. My clothes, my bike, jewelry, dishware, and all personal possessions were strewn everywhere on the lawn. My girlfriend from work came over as we were digging my jewelry out of the dirt. She quietly told me I was coming home with her. I remember feeling scared that I couldn't, but I knew I had to. One night, when Wayne was out drinking, we loaded the truck up, and I left.

As I wanted a normal life, I managed to get married later to a man that didn't abuse me, or so I thought. Just because a man doesn't hit you does not mean you still cannot be abused. My husband managed to control all the finances and make my daughter and I suffer for milk and bread. I went to a friend at work, and I burst out crying because I didn't have money for diapers. I went to the washroom and came back to my desk to see two hundred dollars lying under my keyboard.

I realized I needed to leave my husband. I could not fathom the thought of my daughter seeing the abuse as I had done at her age. I left my marriage when Alyssa was two years old.

That marriage gave me the most beautiful gift in my life, my daughter Alyssa. Throughout the years, I learned to heal myself from this abuse once and for all. In the last five years, I sought out every healing technique I could find to heal my spirit and my soul. I used my native healing to heal the spirit, working in sweat lodges, using ceremonies, and praying to the Great Creator. I worked in a shelter for abused women and children, so I can share my passion. I live to work with women and children today to heal the wounds of tomorrow.

I am now a proud half-Cree woman who lives to stand by my daughter and give her the gift of life. It is my honour to support women in their healing journey, and to know the passion for life that is in my heart. I watch over my mother and sister so that I can hold a space for them, so they can heal their lives after this abuse.

If these stories can touch other women's hearts, we are all sisters. Together we can heal on Grandmother Earth.

> *Patricia M. works in the oil and gas industry in Calgary. She also serves as a board member for a non-profit association. "It is an honour to share my story, not only for my generation, but for all women who share in their healing journey."*

⊞ ⊞ ⊞ ⊞

My Imaginary Chinese Mother
ROBYN LEE HOMELL

Today I am grateful for the life I have been given. I have worked very hard in my fifty-one years to find peace in my soul, and I feel honoured to share part of my story with you.

I was born, as I believe all children are born, a precious new being: a life, an open book, the pages fresh and blank, ready to be filled. Sadly, I was to be abused emotionally, sexually, and physically by my mother and father. I learned that in order to receive any kind of affection from my mother, my little body must endure things that children should never have to face. I learned from my father that fear and obedience were necessary to survive, and that I was worthless enough to deserve the beatings I received. I also learned how to dissociate.

The never-ending assaults on my body, mind, and spirit caused me to find refuge with an imaginary mother, and I would go to her when things were unbearable. There were stories told, and laughed about with relatives, regarding my "Chinese mother."

I remember nothing of our visits together or the wisdom she gave me. It was only in my late forties that I came to appreciate what an incredible gift I had been given. . . .

When my natural mother died of colon cancer, I reached a critical stage in my life. Her last words to me before she died were: "I have always hated you." Unable to cope with that truth either, I slept. I took care of my children, but I lost my spirit to continue. I believe to this day that without my children, I would not have been able to go on. At 325 pounds and emotionally bankrupt, I forced myself into therapy to deal with my abusive marriage and my abuse as a child.

I left my husband at age forty-seven, and went to the Sheriff King women's shelter in Calgary. It was here that I did the majority of the work I needed to do to repair my spirit. I cannot express clearly enough the love and support I found there. They went out of their way to help me, and counselled me for two years after I left. They gave willingly of themselves to my children and me, and helped us start a new life. . . .

It was during my work at Sheriff King that I was once again to discover my "Chinese mother." Several months before leaving my marriage and going to the shelter, I attended a group for sexual abuse healing. I had made a clay sculpture of my spirit guide. I treasured the image that I created with that lump of clay, and kept it with me when I left my marriage. During a discussion about my Chinese mother with my therapist at Sheriff King, it was suggested that I take a trip to the Chinese area in Calgary, and see if I felt any connection. I was to buy some little thing there to honour the memory.

My daughter and I walked around and looked in various shops. I was sad, because I did not feel any real connection. We looked in one last store before we left, and I saw a rainbow of colour on the wall of the shop. It was coming from some crystal ornaments. I have always loved prisms and reflected light, and these reminded me of one I had given to my mother for Christmas years ago. I picked one, and as it was not too expensive, I decided to buy it.

Etched lightly on the ornament was the figure of a woman in the lotus position. It was so like my clay sculpture that I had made out of that lump of clay. I asked the shopkeeper who the woman was. She told me she was Kwan Yin, a Buddhist goddess. I went home, looked her up on the Internet, and I was amazed when I found out Kwan Yin was the goddess of compassion, and the protector of small children.

I realized at that moment how blessed I was, and how I had been loved as a child, not by my biological parents, but a spiritual parent who had taught me things about being a kind and compassionate person. My dissociation had been a gift to help me survive until I could slowly look at the reality as an adult. The director of Sheriff King took my ornament, my sculpture, and my story to a conference on abuse she attended in Victoria. She told me many people were inspired and touched when she read them my story.

I wanted to share it with you now—all the women in Alberta who have had similar stories of abuse, and have struggled to find your way. It is possible to find the love within yourself, and for yourself. We are all worthy of respect.

The most exciting thing that has transpired is the joy of being able to give back to my community. I now volunteer on a crisis line, and I am able to share and give hope to others. I am truly grateful for this. Every time I speak to someone in crisis, I thank every agency, and every person within those agencies, for their support on my quest to become a woman who loves herself, and lives peacefully and happily in the real world. I plan to go back to school next year—yes, even at my age—and take social work, and continue to do work in the community.

In closing, I would like to pay tribute to all the men and women who work so hard to stop the cycle of abuse in their homes and communities.

Their legacy will live on through their children and the generations to follow.

> ❊ *Robyn Lee Homell of Calgary worked in the oil industry as an accountant, and later cared for her children at home. She dedicates this story to the counsellors in Calgary who helped her to recover from childhood trauma and its consequences. She would also like to thank Jackie and George Palmer, "who gave my children and me a safe place to live when we started our new life. Words could never express the gratitude I feel to these amazingly kind and generous people."*

❊ ❊ ❊ ❊

My Daughter Helped Me Most
TERI

I've spent time running to shelters, or talking to people, trying to understand myself, men, and the world around me. I've been frustrated at some of the women who came into my life, full of anger yet unable to objectively do something about their circumstances. I've been angry at the men who offered their "help" in the disguise of need for a mother figure. I've been frustrated with the "help" agencies and some of the people who work in them: the ones who call a person down for being weak, for being in these places. I've had a female social worker tell me that I couldn't receive help if I was sharing a house with a man, unless I was considered common-law with him. Then, from the same worker, I was told that I shouldn't be in a relationship because she thought I was too messed up and couldn't handle it.

I've been told that when I got pregnant with another child, I should have an abortion. And finally I was told that my AISH (disability cheque) was cut down to health care (because since I was living with a man, he could take care of me). So much for any independent try at building my life. I've been told by a number of women what I *should* do, but not to bother them with details on how, or help in a place to stay, or any other way. I should do it all on my own, and not rely on anyone.

It's not that I wanted people to do things for me. I just needed a certain amount of help along the way.

However, I finally pretty much gave up on looking for that help. For me, it seemed if you don't have an education or good health, you are looked down upon and considered a burden. Doesn't matter how much you try, or who you go and see.

Now I just stay at home and survive. Looking for someone to talk to has become a thing of the past. I rely on myself and books and therapy writing. Sometimes I watch motivational programs if they pertain to what I'm thinking about. It's not much, but at least I am away from the negativity out in the world. Now and then an old friend will call or visit, and we can have a decent conversation. There's a certain amount of comfort in knowing the life we grew up in, and accepting one another, without condemnation of each other's lives.

I rely on faith and prayer in the Creator, without going to a church or attending any specific religious group. I've tried that road and it just confused me even more. There are times I wish I could join a women's group, or get more involved in my community, but the injustices out there are just too much for me to handle. I still get angry very easily, and I haven't found out how to direct that anger in a way that is positive and productive.

So I will deal with my adversity in a passive manner until such a time when I can find a way to do something about the things that bother me. I stay at home and look after my daughter. I reflect and try to teach her to be strong from what I've learned, and what I've been through that has made me the strong woman I am today. I try to teach her, not in a negative way, not in anger, but to love and respect herself first.

It has taken me almost forty years to learn that. She has been a large part of my healing, this daughter of mine. I want her to know that.

Teri grew up in northern Alberta near the border of the Northwest Territories, but now lives in a small town in central Alberta. She has worked at a number of jobs—"secretarial mostly, some cooking, ranch help, store clerk, and pretty much anything I could do before my health began to get worse." The mother of six children, she says she enjoys the

*outdoor life, keeping in touch with her Métis/Cree heritage, reading,
and writing. "I find comfort in the written word—it helps me sort out
my thoughts at times."*

❈ ❈ ❈ ❈

My Sister and I

GEORGINA DURAND

Once upon a time, it was sunny and warm,
Two small orphaned girls went to live on a farm
I think of it often, that day in July,
Fate brought us together, my sister and I

Our kinfolk were different, we both looked the same
The same native blood runs through our veins
Two spirits broken, over time we grew fond,
My sister and I, we created a bond

Dust and small whirlwinds, we raced through the fields
We'd lie on the grass, use our hands as a shield,
The sun would sink slowly as we raced the rain clouds
A billowy haze roofed the land like a shroud

Inside we raced to help Dad with his pipe
And we'd sit on the arms of his chair on each side
Weary and tired we slumped off to bed
Safe in the thought of a new day ahead

We dressed under the covers until Dad lit a flame
Sang "Three Little Duckies" when company came
Complacence set in, and I let down my guard,
I forgot my existence when life was so hard

They took her away, I was left on my own
They didn't seem to care I was lost and alone
My sister and I were connected no more
Life ended for me when she walked out that door

Both paths were destined at that fork in the road
The fast lane for her, my anger it showed
My sister was young; for most, easy prey.
Poor judgment was made when they took her away

We each had a life with despair and heartache
Battered and bruised, we both made mistakes.
At times we reached out, and we talked on the phone
My heart filled with joy when she thought to come home.

My life somehow changed, but hers stayed the same.
She would call in the night; her support I became
And I never forgot when we looked to the sky.
The bond that we had, my sister and I . . .

I almost gave up on my sister and I
Until one day she noticed that life passed her by
Recovery was slow, clouds faded and gone,
My sister and I we formed a new bond

Both of our families are grown up and gone
We talk about summers when the sun would beat down
Sobriety for her was like opening a door
My sister and I are together once more

Now we talk on the phone until the sun's in the sky
She gave up the drugs, she has a new high
We disclosed all our secrets, hidden for years
The booze and the drugs, the abuse we endured.

I told her how Daddy took my life in his hands

During an afternoon nap, he made his demands.
She told me her life had been mangled and maimed
Stories of rape and abuse made me ashamed.

I told her I loved her and that I missed all the years
And how after she left, my heart filled with tears.
We cried and we laughed, we both grew so strong.
Till one day she said: "I think something's wrong."

I didn't want to listen, I covered my ears.
How can this be happening? I yelled through my tears.
"Now, don't you cry, sis. I'm going to beat the Big C,
And we'll still be together, you just wait and see!"

And she fought and she fought, and I cried every day
I couldn't bear the thought of her going away
And she didn't even know, she died while she slept
And I questioned my God, and I silently wept.

They say that it's darkest just before the dawn
And it took me some time to accept that she's gone
But she did feel my love when her life finally ceased
And I take comfort in knowing she's finally at peace.

> *Georgina Durand of Edmonton wrote this poem for her foster sister Ramona. "In our early years we were the best of friends," she writes. "We were brought to this little house on the prairie in Alberta when we were both five years old. We both had Native blood, and although we were raised by an old Irish couple along with other foster kids, we both had the Native spirit. Mona got pregnant when she was fifteen, and our lives changed. She took one path, and I took another."*
>
> *Georgina sent the first part of this poem to her foster sister when Ramona discovered she had cancer. "She read it over and over again." Her sister died three months later.*

❀   ❀   ❀   ❀

My Daughter Saved My Life

JUANITA MURPHY

On the night I was in the police station, sitting in a cell, I could hear my daughter crying for me.

It was then I realized that I needed to change, because I really did love my daughter. I wanted to be a mother to her. Not just a drug-addicted mom, but the best mom in the world. I knelt down on the floor and asked God for a sign of hope. Just then a welfare worker walked in and told me the hard truth. I would lose my daughter for good if I didn't clean up and get off the dope. She told me that I could be killed on the street or I would end up killing myself, and my daughter would have no mother. Just like me. I had no mother. She eventually killed herself and I found her dead body. It is a horror I will never forget. That picture of my dead mother is fresh in my mind always and forever. I didn't want my daughter to be living with that same picture in her memory.

The welfare worker took my hand, and told me I can change. She said she would help me if I asked. I did ask for help that night. I realized I couldn't do it alone. I needed child welfare. I stretched out my arms and reached for help. My life has never been the same since.

Child welfare workers stayed that night, and were in my home for three days around the clock. They came to my home every two days for months. I had to work hard and go to parenting courses and learn how to be a parent. I went to a budgeting course so I could learn how not to waste money, and use it properly. I had to prove to my daughter that I could go to the washroom, and come back out straight. She wouldn't let me close the bathroom door for a long time. I had to prove to her that I would stay home. She followed me everywhere. Child welfare workers gave me the tools to work with, and the support. I did the work, and today I have been clean for seven years.

I tell this story so someone will read this and realize that they too are making the same mistake I did. This story has a happy ending. Your story might not have a happy ending if you don't quit living a destructive way of life. You are not only hurting yourself, you are hurting your children. Nobody asked to be your children. They didn't ask to be raised by abusive or addicted parents. So please give your seed a chance to grow strong and healthy. Give them love and support so they will grow into beautiful human beings.

I'd like to thank the welfare worker who saw life in me. She showed me that I could love. She showed me that I could be a loving and healthy mother to my kids.

I would like to thank my daughter for her unconditional love. She stuck with me through all my troubles and rough times. She is still with me today. She is a survivor. She is my role model. I can truly say my daughter saved my life. She showed me that life can change if you really want it to. I can love myself, and I can love life. I loved enough to have a loving son who was spared the hell that she lived. We are free and happy.

I forgive my mother and father. I know that there was something in their lives that went terribly wrong. They were teaching their children what someone taught them. People treat others the way they were treated, so somewhere in their lives they, too, were being abused. They did drugs and alcohol to kill the pain. Like me, they were trying to kill a bad memory. If they had had a good life, then maybe I would have had a good life, too. They were repeating the cycle that was taught to them.

I tell this story so I can encourage you to break the chain. Give your next generation a chance to live a good life. I am a believer in breaking the chain.

❖ *This is an excerpt from Juanita Murphy's longer story in which she describes an abusive childhood in foster homes and group homes, which led to child prostitution and drug addiction. "I started to hate before I loved. I turned my first trick at twelve years old to feed myself. It didn't stop at one trick. I had to feed myself every day. . . ."*

She reflects: "I cannot go back and change what I did, but I can change the future, so I can live longer to be with my kids. I wanted to give my children, and their children, a good chance at living a good life, free from alcohol and drugs. I love my kids. They are my life and heart-beat. I am proud of myself for making the change, and my children are safe and happy."

Juanita has worked in the restaurant industry for four years. "I am thirty-seven years old, and glad to be alive. I am raising my two children, and I volunteer at the Prostitution Awareness and Action Foundation of Edmonton to help others."

⊞ ⊞ ⊞ ⊞

A Tribute to My Sister

PAMELA KLEIN

My sister, my best friend
Our love will never end
In the mirror there are two
Our bright eyes are the same hue

Yet a difference stands out
Confidence versus self-doubt
How did this happen? How can it be?
Same genes, same family tree

He is responsible, this I know,
Controlling even when you say, "No!"
Your spirit, so easy to crush,
With words. Now tell him to hush

I admire your great strength
Your patience, and to what lengths
You will go for your young son
His well-being is priority number one

A happy home he has to know
Things aren't right, you decide to go
Start again, embark on a new life
Simply as you, not somebody's wife.

For many years you heal your wounds
Rebuild your life that feels like ruins
Finally you are ready again to date
Ready to accept your personal fate

Another single parent you meet
On the same page, now that's a feat!
Life is rosy and good
Way to go, girl! It should!

You deserve a life full of hope
Not just: "I think I can cope"
But wait. Something has gone terribly wrong.
This marriage is over—he's gone.

His own wounds were never healed
Buried deep, no layers peeled
"Failure again!" you cry out
Filled with betrayal and more self-doubt

"How can this happen?" you ask. "Why me?"
Had God not set your weary heart free?
Again there is misery and woe
Once a lover, now only your foe

Was there something you missed?
Something that hadn't been fixed?
Ignore the gossip, there is no scandal,
There isn't anything you can't handle

Forget him. Forget his lies
Now is the time to be wise
Take a long look in the mirror
Beyond the pain and the fear

See the woman you are,

She was never too far.
Love yourself, not the man,
This was always God's plan.

For my sister, my twin!
I knew you would win!

Pamela Klein of Red Deer dedicates this poem to her sister. Pamela has published two suspense novels and a resource book for parents of newly diagnosed deaf children.

"This poem is especially dear to my heart, for it reflects some of the challenges and triumphs my sister, and best friend, has faced throughout her adult life," she adds. "I'm sure many women will identify with her struggles."

⁂ ⁂ ⁂ ⁂

Inheritance
ANONYMOUS

In the course of life, daughters inherit their mothers' stories, sometimes reluctantly. When the strongest thread in the story is family violence, inspiration is hard to come by. It can be a long and layered struggle to become an inspiration, and to become inspired. I have found both. . . .

Admittedly, in my childhood I concentrated on my mother's flaws rather than her strengths. Amid the heartache of home, I could not see that my mother was hardworking, honest, responsible, resourceful, and independent. I could only see that she did not protect me. It did not matter to me then that she coped with isolated northern conditions. It did not matter that she had to walk, take a freighter down the river, fly in an airplane, and then take a truck into civilization to deliver her children. It did not matter that she stayed home to raise those same children. It did not matter that while doing so, she educated herself at a distance because my father had cancer.

I now know the truth. These things did matter. I have learned that public accomplishments can overshadow a different kind of success so that the quiet unfolding and expansion of another human being is easily lost. Sadly, I have measured my mother this way. In doing so, I have not welcomed her painful growth with appropriate awe for her achievements.

Over the years she has transformed tears into strength. Slowly, denial gave way to self-awareness. Submission became courage. Uncertainty was replaced by decisiveness. Silence found a voice. Obedience questioned long-held beliefs. Despair gave way to possibility. Salvation replaced security. And always, fear sought courage, knowing it was always someplace within. . . .

Like the rest of society, I often wondered why she didn't just leave. Of course, she did leave. Many times, in fact. And on one such occasion I vividly recall the phone call she received from my grandmother. I listened in on the extension. My grandmother was angry and blaming. You did not leave marriages, no matter how abusive. Even at the age of eighty, with full knowledge of the pain and crisis in the relationships of her six adult children, my grandmother was adamant in her denial.

At first glance, ending an abusive marriage does not seem so inspiring. However, it is not simply about ending the abuse. Rather, it is about ending years of pain and fear, years of denial, years of generational abuse and dysfunction. It is about reaching for and claiming a new life even when you have been conditioned otherwise. It is about uprooting an entire family tree.

I have learned to look into private places, in quiet rooms, behind closed doors. Such unseen activity should be the standard of heroic measure. I have seen many things in my mother: compassion, humility, peace, generosity, faith, and love. She has sewn quilts for the homeless. She has apologized for her mistakes and wrestled with the consequences. She has prayed every day. She has taught abuse prevention to classrooms of adolescents. She has sat beside those preparing to die. She has continued to love and nurture her husband through separations and reconciliation. . . .

As daughters of family violence, there is so much standing in our way. We are left wanting, looking everywhere aimlessly and endlessly.

Until finally we discover, most painfully, the inheritance.

Finally we can begin sorting through the story that has become our own. Slowly, carefully, we sift through pain and joy, fear and love, hope and despair. We are faced with the enormous process of healing. At some point along the path, we are challenged to forgive our mothers and ourselves. The very act of forgiveness can split your heart in two. At first it feels like it is breaking, but really it is opening a heart that has been systematically shut down. . . .

In many ways my life is a reflection of my mother's influence, although our paths were not always parallel. In fact, we have taken turns being the mother in this relationship. Like her, I work hard. I am resourceful. I am independent. I love my father, and I stretch to meet him in a positive relationship. I question things and challenge injustice in all its forms. I have strong faith and reach for the divine every day, and I am committed to personal growth and to helping others heal.

After years of struggle, we now enjoy a happier life, a healthier life, free of the weighting of family violence. In the end, the most important genealogical accounting is that someday my daughter will inherit a new story.

The author is a social worker and health professional. She is exploring the relationship between spirituality and health in her graduate studies. She lives in Edmonton.

❁ ❁ ❁ ❁

Patricia and Her Daughter
MOTHER'S STORY

My name is Patricia, and I am an intimate abuse survivor. I am also a mom, grandmother, friend, and buddy, in addition to being a recovering alcoholic with thirty-three months of sobriety.

I was in a long-term relationship with my abuser, who practiced all forms of abuse: mental, physical, sexual, financial, spiritual. All the factors led to me and my children taking refuge at the Brenda Strafford Centre in Calgary.

As I write this letter, in a strange way, I am sad to tell you my abuser died of his own hand on August 17, 2003. So I should be free, but I am not. You are never free of the emotional or sexual abuse that is done to you. Physical abuse fades, and so do the bruises, but the psychological scars never do. To this day, even with the help I have received, I can feel the gut-wrenching pain. This was the most destructive relationship of my life. I loved this person dearly, but I also hated him. It was a relationship of adulation entwined with degradation. A time of intense pleasure, followed by unbelievable pain. It was in this time that I lost the essence of who I once was.

While living at Brenda Strafford Centre, I learned to take back parts of my life. The abusive relationship is so dynamic and deadly at times; it sometimes teaches the abused to finally strike back, when that act is so out of character. . . . Many times we are not able to elude our abuser, so we seek refuge at a place such as BSC.

At times I find it hard to live in my skin, but the strength and support I receive enables me to move on. I am one of the truly lucky ones who got to come out the other side, and not lose my life. The staff at BSC loved me and my kids to life and health.

I am not sure if this is going to help someone, but I truly hope so. Enclosed is a poem my younger daughter wrote in her tears and fear.

We need to be there for all who are being abused: men, women, elders, and children.

DAUGHTER'S POEM
I've seen it all
I've been through it all
The abuse, the drugs, the alcohol
I used to cry myself to sleep
Waking up with my mom's blood on the rug
The pain, the emptiness, the dark
Being alone

I was so scared when he walked in the door
It was all going to happen again
It starts with the emotional abuse
Then the physical
Something I hated the most
He would hit her and I would panic
Usually it was not my fault
He once was the best thing in my mom's life
Then she became his wife
That is when he started to pull knives
Cops were always at our house
Not only for him, but also for my sister,
A heavy drug user, and her boyfriend, also an abuser,
As I watched this, I grew not only physically but also emotionally
I learned I do not need him as a dad
When I have the world's
Greatest MOM!

> *A mother and daughter submitted this story and poem to* Standing Together *through a counselor, Norine King, at the Brenda Strafford Centre in Calgary.*

My Mother's Fight

DIANA BLISS

When I was growing up, I would make jokes about how the spacing of my siblings and I was determined by my mother's letting my father come back into our home. He married my mother and left just after getting her pregnant with my brother. He returned long enough for my mother to have two more children. He could not stand being around all that responsibility, so he left again.

The community ostracized my mother because she was alone with three children. It was the 1950s and even though everyone knew that my father had left, and taken his income with him, they still refused to talk to her or help in any way. She took him back again long enough for two more babies, and then he left again. She took him back, and my younger brother came along. See? My mother taking my father back determined the spacing.

When I grew up and began to piece together the events of my childhood, I realized just how difficult my mother's life had been. Each time my father left, he left her destitute. He took the only income. She went to welfare often, and on one occasion in the late 1950s, we were put into foster care. When my father was living with us, there was so much yelling that I cannot actually remember him not yelling at someone. He left for the last time when I was nine.

He came home angry about God only knows what, and started yelling at my mother. Supper was not on the table fast enough for him, but he had failed to give her the money she needed to buy any groceries. When my older brother tried to stop him from hurting my mother, my father started in on him. Then my sisters got involved, and he seemed to be attacking anyone randomly. My sister pushed us little ones into the bedroom and closed the door. He stomped through the house, yelling, hitting, and yelling some more. When my sister tried to call the police, he tore the telephone off the kitchen wall.

At the age of nine I was so accustomed to the fighting that I left the bedroom for something to eat. In the kitchen, while my father tore at the phone and yelled, I stood and watched passively. I knew exactly how far away to stand so that I would not get hurt. I knew the boundaries of his fits. I knew that as long as I did not cross those lines, he would not see me.

Later my sister ran out of the house to the neighbours to call the police. It was about four in the morning or so, maybe later. He had not stopped yelling, not even for a minute. He had not stopped storming through the house, hitting anything and anyone who got too close. I was back in the bedroom by then. It was easy; just wait until he stormed into another room, and follow a safe distance behind. No problem for a nine-year-old.

When the officer arrived, my father fought with him. One Mountie, twice my father's size, had to wrestle him to the ground and put handcuffs on him. I watched from the bedroom door. When my father was finally subdued, I ran to the window that looked out on the otherwise quiet suburban street. I watched the Mountie escort my father to his waiting cruiser. I watched as he put my father in the back seat. My father was quiet and walked obediently beside the officer. I watched the cruiser drive away into the night. I watched the silent street, and wondered what other people were doing in their houses. For many years I assumed that they were all doing what we were doing: fighting, yelling, watching their fathers beat their mothers. It did not dawn on me until I was an adult that there was anything wrong or even unusual about how our house functioned.

As far as I know, the police released him the next day. He never came home again. I never missed him as a father. We had to turn to welfare. Our neighbours would not let us play with their children once they found out our dad had left. My mother tried to find a job to support us, but many employers told her they would not hire a married woman. Once, she asked during an interview, "Why not?" The answer she got was that her husband should be supporting her. Eventually she found a job as a teacher, but only because there was such a shortage of teachers, and they were prepared to hire anybody. She tried to file for divorce on grounds of abandonment, but the court clerk and her lawyer, who did not seem to want to bother with her, told her she had to find him before she could file for divorce. She went to the police to file a missing person report, but they told her she had to file for divorce first. She gave up for many years.

My mother suffered years of abuse from my father. Each of the children has suffered because of his abuse. We were in terrible poverty in a world that did not care, and often blamed my mother for the situation.

However, my mother also found her own willingness to fight. Welfare told her she had to move out of her house, and she fought to stay. "The only houses I can afford are in terrible neighbourhoods," she told them. "I want my children to stay where they will be safe." It took guts for her to argue the point, because at that time a welfare recipient could not hold a mortgage. She proved to them that it was cheaper for them to let her stay where she was. My mother fought to keep us in school. She fought, and ultimately won. All of us but one grew up, and all of us got to college, with one exception. My oldest sister has been a missing person since the mid-1970s.

My mother was eventually able to go to university. She earned two degrees from the University of Calgary. I am married now with children of my own, and I am finding that I must fight for their needs. I learned to fight from my mother.

■ *Diana Bliss, a writer, lives in Calgary with her husband and three children. She reports that her mother, who prefers to remain anonymous, began to attend university at the age of fifty-five, and subsequently earned two degrees. She has remarried a man "so good to her that we all refer to him as our father. He has given her all the love and caring that my father never did."*

⊠ ⊠ ⊠ ⊠

My Mother's Lesson: Learn To Love Yourself

ELEANOR LABOUCAN

My mother's name is Bertha Anderson Laboucan. She is a mother, friend, and grandmother, and a role model to many women. If there were one word to describe my mother, it would be warrior. I say this because despite her abusive upbringing and violent marriage, she has managed to achieve many successes in her life. She is a First Nations woman whom I can envision as a future elder because of her personal attributes, and the humility she shows in her personal and professional life.

She was born June 18, 1956, in a small Métis settlement 460 kilometres northeast of Edmonton. She is the second oldest of seven children. My mother has five children, four boys and me. There are two sides to my mother: one is her passive, quiet, gentle side, and the other is her strong sense of social justice. She has always tried to advocate for what society calls the underdogs, people who are oppressed by racism, poverty, discrimination, and violence. As a child growing up, there were many occasions when I went with my mother to help those who suffered from alcoholism, poverty, and mental illness. Many times I watched her stay up late at night to write a letter of advocacy for those who were being treated unjustly.

My mother always told me there are life lessons to learn from. Whenever she comes across obstacles in her life, she has a firm belief in a written quote she carries around in her pocket: *If the Creator brings you to it, he will see you through it.* This is the idea she falls back on whenever she is troubled. She talks with fondness about her grandmother, who taught her kindness, love, caring and honesty. Her grandma had strong Catholic beliefs. One of the beliefs she passed on to my mother was to love thy neighbour, and to continue to love those who hurt you. She says if you only love those who love you back, you don't get as many rewards as when you learn to love those who have hurt or harmed you in any way.

I vaguely remember some of the things that happened in my home as I was growing up, although some memories are vivid. I asked my mother to share the vivid recollections with me so that I can share hope and faith with other women who face similar situations. What I want to say is that violence is a continuing cycle, which leaves women feeling like victims, and that can manifest itself in various situations throughout our lives if we do not learn to recognize this feeling within ourselves.

I have learned from my mother that women can break away from violence, through help from different agencies such as a women's shelter, acquiring education, and using our own traditional helping systems as First Nations people. As she talks about her childhood abuse, she has long since realized that violence is a cycle, and that her mother had most likely adopted certain abusive patterns from her own family of origin.

I begin this writing with my mother's stories as she remembers them.

This is a verbatim transcript of her stories. Her most vivid memory of abuse began in her childhood.

Bertha's story: I am eight years old. I have been standing at the top of the hill outside my grandmother's house now for a few hours. In the dark I can see headlights from a distance, with endless vehicles heading home from town on a Friday night. Each time I see a vehicle approaching, I leap, wishing and praying it is my parents' vehicle. At midnight they still had not arrived to pick us up from Grandma's. My younger siblings and I ended up sleeping on the floor of my grandmother's house. I woke up early, anxious to go home, wondering if my parents brought home any candy for us. As I was walking home, a part of me was hesitant, wondering what I would find. As usual, when I walked through the door there was still a roaring party with the stereo going full blast. There was an inch of mud caked into the linoleum, and beer bottles scattered all over the floor and lined on the coffee tables. My immediate reaction was to get a pail of water with a rag. I got down on my hands and knees to start picking up the bottles and clean up so that when Mom woke up, she wouldn't be so angry with Dad. I started washing the floor, trying to block out the deafening noise of dozens of people talking at the same time in slurry voices. Some of the drunks noticed a little girl trying to wash the floor amidst people dancing drunkenly. They tried to move her out of the way.

As the supply of beer started to dwindle, the drunks started to disperse and leave. I kept wishing they wouldn't go, because I knew what would happen when they left. My father would pick a fight with my mother, and he would start to hit her or push her. When this happened, I would push my way between them, and push my father away, begging him to stop. Sometimes my mother would flee with my siblings to hide in the bush when my father started in on her.

On one occasion my mother forgot the wallet, which contained all the money, under the mattress. My mother told me to sneak back into the house to retrieve it. As I approached the house, I saw my father sitting on the steps of the pumphouse, loading a shotgun. I went and sat beside him, and asked him what he was doing. I don't remember what he said to me. I told him I was going inside the house. As soon as I got inside the house, I took the wallet and ran through the back door and down the hill, running as fast as I could back to my mother. It did not occur to me that my father could have easily shot me in his drunken state. I realize now, in retrospect, how little I valued my life, because my mother apparently did not care whether I lived or died. I was not important to her.

After each weekend of my father's binge drinking, my mother would verbally abuse him throughout the week. Often, in her rage, she would misdirect her anger at me, and hit me or pull my hair. To compound things and make my life more miserable, my older sister would find ways to get me in trouble, so my mother would have a reason to hit me. My father would often stick up for me and tell my mother not to be so hard on me, and this only made my mother more abusive towards me.

I started reading at an early age so I could seek solace and comfort in reading about people who had wonderful lives. I lived vicariously through the characters in the stories; I read everything I could put my hands on. I read while I cleaned, while I ate, and even while walking to school. Every day after school I had to do chores: washing dishes, sweeping, chopping wood, and hauling water. One day my mother came across the stacked magazines I had hidden under the bed. In her rage, she stuffed them in the wood stove. She said I spent too much time reading, and not enough time on my chores. She also said, "You don't need school. All you need is a husband."

At the age of fourteen I met a boy who later became my husband. I was starved for love and affection. I was willing to do anything to keep this man who professed to love me. At age seventeen, I deliberately became pregnant in an effort to escape the home life that was becoming increasingly unbearable.

By the time I had my fifth child, my life was again unbearable. The life that I thought would me much better than my life with my family of origin, was worse. Some of the excerpts of my married life are as follows. . . .

Another lonely weekend with the kids, and I was pacing the floor, wondering where my husband was. I was going to be late for work. I needed the truck to get to work. Just when I was ready to call in sick, I heard a truck outside. I peeked out the window and saw him and two of his friends. I had a sinking feeling as he walked in. I could see he had been drinking. "I need the truck for work," I said. He started to raise his voice, and said, "My friends are waiting in the truck, and I'm going to use it." I said, "You will scare the children with your screaming; we can talk in the bedroom." I was walking to the bedroom when he came in from behind me and slammed the door shut. He said, "You f——ing bitch, you're going to get it." He lunged at me, and wrapped his hands around my neck. I started screaming. I was feeling light-headed, while black dots were swimming in front of my eyes. As I was blacking out, I heard my sister kick the door open, and I could hear her screaming at him, and pulling his hands away from my neck. When I came to, he had left with the truck.

After he left, I confided to my sister that I was afraid to leave my husband for fear that I could not make it in life alone. She quickly pointed out that I had been struggling alone for most of my marriage. It took some time for me to digest this information. By this time my self-esteem was shot. My feeling of worthlessness was so ingrained from my childhood, and now with my marriage. After hearing how dumb and stupid, fat and ugly, I was for most of my marriage, I felt I needed someone in my life to affirm who I was.

At this time I did not have a firm sense of myself. As time passed I became depressed; but I could see the children's behaviour changed whenever their dad was around. One day my oldest son, Garry, came to me, crying, "I don't want Dad to live with us." I was shocked when he said that, as I had always believed that children needed a father. I was raised with the belief that you made your bed, so lie in it. In other words, you stay in your marriage for better or worse. I pondered for a long time what my son told me, and I believe that became a turning point in my marriage. The next time my husband left us to go philandering, I went to apply for a restraining order for him to stay away from us.

I felt somewhat relieved that I did not have to endure his drunken episodes and his sexual abuse towards me. Being alone, and realizing I had made a decision to raise the children by myself, gave me strength. I realized he had been sucking the strength and energy out of me, and was pulling me back from using my own inner strength. By now I realized that if I was to provide the children with a decent life, I had to become educated. Soon after, I enrolled in college to complete my first degree.

Eleanor's story: As I watched my mother dressed in her traditional outfit, carrying a feather across the stage to receive her Master's degree in education, I realized how strong she was, and how much sacrifice she had made to get to where she was.

She recalls a time when she was asked to speak to a group of Aboriginal women at a women's shelter, and one woman asked her, "How did you get to where you are?" She laughed and replied, "I owe it to my husband." They asked her, "Did he support you while you were going to school?" She said, "No, my husband abused and cheated on me."

I often wonder what it was that gave my mother the strength to overcome all of the obstacles and hardships of raising five of us alone, and still attain three university degrees, including her Master's degree in education. When I asked her that question, she said, "I learned to love myself. I learned who I was as an Aboriginal woman, by learning from elders and living a traditional way of life."

Today my mother attends sweats and cultural events, and she continues to seek guidance from elders. She constantly tries to live and model the natural laws of strength, honesty, sharing, and caring in her personal and professional life. Her current work is dedicated to First Nations education, integrating traditional knowledge into the curriculum for Aboriginal children. . . .

Hearing my mother's stories of her past fills me with confusion, anger, and sadness. If I could erase all of her hurt and pain, I would in a heartbeat. However, I also realize that these experiences have enabled her to grow stronger. Today, when she tells me stories, or gives me advice, I listen with all my heart. I wonder what would have happened if my mother stayed with my father. That thought makes me cringe, because deep down I know the abuse would not have stopped. As my mother describes her feelings of helplessness and hopelessness, I know exactly how she feels, for I came to experience the same violence and abuse from my common-law spouse not too long ago.

I never thought it would happen to me. I always thought I was stronger and smarter because of my mother's experiences. As a teenager I had vowed I would never allow any man to raise a hand towards me. And then one night it happened while he was drinking. He lost control, and began to punch me in the face. I remember feeling this deep fear well up inside me. I was so scared he might not stop punching and choking me.

I was frozen with disbelief that this was actually happening to me. When the cops arrived, there was blood all over me. The police escorted me safely out so I could call my mother.

The first thing she did was to give me a hug, and tell me I was safe and to come and stay with her until I decided what to do. That was six months ago. I have never looked back. To this day, I still have nightmares of my common-law spouse punching me over and over again.

I have come to realize that it is no accident that I was born into my family of origin. I, too, have lessons to learn, and it is these life lessons that enable me to understand violence and its long-term effects.

I offer a few lines from a poem by a Lakota Chief, Yellow Lark, and I dedicate it to all women.

Oh, Great Spirit,
whose voice I hear in the winds
and whose breath gives life to all the world,
hear: I am small and weak
I need your strength and wisdom . . .

I seek strength, not to be greater than my brother,
but to fight my greatest enemy, myself.
Make me always ready to come to you
with clean hands and straight eyes
so when life fades as the fading sunset
my spirit may come to you without shame.

Hiy Hiy
In peace and friendship,
Eleanor Laboucan

Eleanor Laboucan has worked as an overnight care worker at a women's emergency shelter in Edmonton. "I am currently going back to university to attain my Health Administration degree, and I hope to do more community work."

Most of All

JOANNA (JO) FOSTER

During my youth
thankful for hope and new beginnings
years of hardship, poverty, wishing, praying,
my mother's courage amidst past terror
her calm shining through . . .

I grew up like two women
happy to be alive and survive
thankful to be home again
surrounded by
my grandmother's teachings
my mother's being
their strength, their love
we struggled to get by
our years became full,
determination, peace, a safe place
immersed in light and encouragement
I began to believe in myself
with the guidance of two women
I believed life could be different

through years of ups and downs
perseverance, and deep inside, a happy heart,
I became a leader, a role model, a good mother, a storyteller . . .
First one in my family with a degree,
and life's experiences of hard work paid off, "with distinction"
because of the love of two women
my mother
my grandmother

I watched
they worked their fingers to the bone
always with kindness, and a smile,

and pleased with life's simple pleasures,
caring for each other,
family came first

because of two women
I am inspired
I can love
I am strong
I dream, take action
I am fulfilled, I feel

My dearest two women are gone now
And yet, reminded of our happy times,
I gain strength through my loss
They live within me now,
My heart, full of joy, is ready to help myself and others
To be: most of all.

Jo Foster of Edmonton wrote this tribute shortly after the death of her mother, Veronica Catherine Saban, remembering her courage and hope. The mother of two sons, Jo looks to the lives of her late mother and grandmother for inspiration. She says she believes in the value of "genuine empathy, hope, helping others to have a voice, and providing them with support in making their goals and dreams come true."

My Grandmother's Recipe for Success

AMANDA JEAN LOVIG

My grandmother, Jean Paré, was an excellent cook right from the beginning. Growing up during the Great Depression, she would experiment in the kitchen and regularly impress her parents and siblings with freshly baked concoctions and delicious home-cooked meals. Even when food was scarce and some ingredients were rare, my grandmother knew just what to use to keep the final result flavourful and appetizing.

Despite being Canada's most popular cookbook author today, my grandmother is no slave to recipe instructions. She knows when to follow the rules, and when to break them. In 1981, when she wrote her first cookbook and broke into publishing, it was her blissful ignorance that brought her quick success. In an industry where five thousand copies of a book sold is considered a bestseller, Jean had fifteen thousand copies of her first cookbook printed, before anyone had agreed to buy them! Fortunately, her recipes were highly sought after by her catering customers. It didn't take long for her cookbook to become a hit, flying off the shelves, demanding a reprint and additional cookbook titles in the series.

Instead of following the regular publishing rules—only approaching bookstores to sell her cookbooks—Jean decided to pitch to managers at grocery stores, hardware stores, and even a beauty parlour and an ice cream parlour. She knew her cookbooks would sell wherever the people were, and she was right! Today she is the co-founder of Company's Coming Publishing Limited, and has sold twenty-two million cookbooks.

Things weren't always as easy as pie.

In the 1960s, Jean was a single mother of four children with no job and no home. Not wanting to ask for help from her parents, she set up camp—literally—with her two youngest at a campground on the outskirts of Vermilion, Alberta. And that's where she stayed until it was too cold to keep sleeping in a tent.

Then she and her children moved to an unheated log cabin for the fall, and a dismal rental apartment for the winter. These were my grandmother's darkest days, because she wanted her children to be happy, and she wanted to make a new life for herself. Times were hard, but she remembered her father's advice to her as a child: *Just get going, and do it.* And so she did.

Jean managed to persuade a local banker to take a chance on her cooking. With the help of a loan, Jean took over and managed the Rio Café in downtown Vermilion. Despite the promised financial independence, the popular diner also came with all the headaches of staff issues and the incredibly long work hours, taking her away from her kids. So Jean decided to sell the Rio in order to concentrate on what she did best: catering. The diner did bring her one special, regular customer—Larry Paré, a local electrical contractor whom Jean married in July of 1968.

Soon my grandmother's catering business was a success. She earned a place in the hearts of her fellow townspeople as the caterer whose only instructions were most often: "Jean, will you handle it?" The inspiration for Jean to create the Company's Coming cookbook series came from the empty plates following every catering function, coupled with the outpouring of requests for her recipes.

My grandmother has not forgotten her past challenges. She has never taken her success for granted. Her priority today is to give to those less fortunate, and to share her wealth and success with others.

Travelling to Haiti together in 2002, my grandmother and I had the rare experience of meeting a few children that we sponsored through Foster Parents Plan and World Vision Canada. In that place so far away, no one recognized her face or knew her role in Canadian kitchens or retail stores. Still, they honoured her with food, songs, and thankful prayers for her financial sponsorship and letter writing over the years. You know, they've kept every letter she's ever mailed? They affectionately call her Mommy Jean.

It is in these rare moments here in Canada, or halfway around the world, that I realize how down-to-earth she's always been, and how brave she was to overcome the adversity in her life. She created something deliciously successful when most might have given up.

My grandmother's recipe for success has not exactly been traditional, but she has relied on hard work, perseverance, optimism, creativity, ingenuity, and compassion. They have yielded excellent results. I wish to honour this remarkable woman, and inspire others with her story because they, too, possess the recipe for success.

Amanda Jean Lovig works in her grandmother's business, Company's Coming Publishing Ltd. She lives in Edmonton.

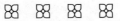

Sisters of Sorrow

JOEY HAMELIN

I dedicate my collection of poems to all grandmothers, mothers, and daughters who have been affected by incarceration.

From the eyes of a child, life was simple. I was happy under the customary care of my Cree grandparents. Life was about survival and simplicity, and not about material possessions. I thank the Creator for my deep-rooted relationship with my grandparents. These early teachings about values and philosophies were invaluable as I began to learn about the historical injustices experienced by our peoples, including the life of my mother.

A spirited Cree woman, she gave me up for a life of adventure in a strange world filled with resistance to residential school, rebellion against racism, street life, heroin, and ultimately Kingston Penitentiary for Women, as evidenced by the tattoos on her arms, and her absence in our lives.

In her spirit, my grandmother reaches out to you as a mother whose daughter runs wild with the wind. As daughter to her daughter, I have come to understand the gift of family, and that we must give our love to our children—no matter what! This is truly unconditional love, pure love. The Creator plans for us to love our children, no matter what. As parents and grandparents, this is our purpose. Our children are our teachers. Miles apart, with pure love and in true spirit, my grandmother and mother climbed hills of hope, change, and steep mountains of challenge. . . In her own voice, my grandmother, Josephine, speaks to you . . .

> Sometimes stuff happens
> Sit quietly, if it happened to me
> It can happen to you
> In gentleness I ask for your friendship
>
> Life continues as I step into the land of darkness
> It tastes like poison—sorrow, grief, and shame
> I see my sisters and they are still standing . . .

Joey Hamelin is a senior policy advisor with the Ministry of Children's Services in Alberta. A mother and grandmother, she says she enjoys "a rustic lifestyle on a small chunk of land outside Edmonton." This excerpt is a short introduction to Joey's longer collection of poems written in the voice of her late grandmother. "In life, we have hope," she says. "In family, we are truly blessed. Thank you, Creator."

⌗ ⌗ ⌗ ⌗

Walking Toward a Better Life

ANONYMOUS

As I walked along the wall, and down the street
I paused, and was astounded at what I saw
There on the street lay a child's teddy bear:
torn, tattered, dirty, and ragged.
A sign that something may have gone wrong,
Or just a toy forgotten.

I walked further down the street, and around the corner
When I paused this time, I saw a little girl crying
I was in complete wonderment and confusion

As I continued down the street, I found a young mother:
Lonely, tattered, torn, dirty, and ragged
Just like the teddy bear

As I continued down the street
I paused one more time
An older woman was lying on the sidewalk
She looks lifeless and abused. She appeared to be shot

I then turned and looked into the reflection I saw in the window
Suddenly I realized the woman on the sidewalk was me

I looked back up the street, realizing my life had passed before me
A life of sadness, abuse, and destruction

Then I awoke, gripping a teddy bear
I looked into my child's eyes and decided
I have to break the cycle of abuse and destruction

I have been living like my mother and grandmother
It has to stop with me, here and now.
I am the only one who can do it
For my daughter's sake I have to break the cycle

My child depends on me for a safe, healthy upbringing
Please let us show our children a different life.
Let's stop the abuse with us.
It is all in our hands.
We can do it, one person at a time.

"I will always stand on my own two feet and support myself," writes the anonymous author of this poem. She supported her family as a waitress through two abusive marriages, and after she was hospitalized for severe physical injuries. "For everything we have been through, we have survived," she says. After her second divorce, she raised three "healthy and well-behaved children" to adulthood as a single parent, and then found new happiness in a friendship with a peaceful man. "We love each other, and each other's children," she says. "Please withhold my name. I am still very afraid of my ex-husband."

❀ ❀ ❀ ❀

Joyce

CARMYN BLOCK

I want to tell you of a very ordinary woman who has done extraordinary things in her life. She is my mother, and she amazes me. Her name is Joyce, and she is the eldest of six daughters born to a farming family. She worked hard with her family to make the farm a success. When Joyce was fourteen, she left home to go to school in town. Until then she had been educated in a small country school. Joyce graduated from high school at sixteen years of age, and then went to teacher's college for one year.

Joyce began to teach at the age of seventeen. She had a contract with a school to teach for two years as they helped pay for her education. When Joyce was twenty, she met a man who was adventurous and a little dangerous. They became a couple and were married in July. Their first daughter was born that September. Two other daughters followed in short succession.

Joyce went back to teaching shortly after her youngest daughter was born. One day she came home from work to find that her husband had left. She packed up the girls, and hitchhiked back to her family. Joyce and the girls stayed there for a while to regroup, and then she made the decision to go back to school and get her teaching degree. Everyone packed up and moved to the big city, where the family lived in a two-bedroom apartment.

When Joyce earned her teaching certificate, she moved the girls to a small farming community in order to teach Grade 1. She taught in that school until she retired at the age of fifty-five.

Now you may think that this is an interesting story, but so what? A lot of women have worked while raising their children. It is important to remember that the time was the early 1960s. She was the only single parent in the community, and was not always welcomed. There were many times when she was excluded because she was single. It was also during this time that Joyce went back to school to complete her degree, graduating when her youngest daughter was twelve. At one point Joyce was going to school, teaching school, and raising three girls by herself. She also found the time to bake homemade bread and sew clothes for the family.

There were many nights when she would go to bed after midnight, only to get up at five to start her day.

Joyce is a strong woman, and raised her daughters to be strong. She raised them to expect to be educated and successful. When her husband finally came back to be with the family, eight years had passed. He came back to four women. Her husband was not a happy man and expressed that through binge drinking and violence. He would be sober for months, and then go drinking and come home swinging. Joyce would do everything she could to protect her daughters from his violence. There were no shelters close, and the extended family and community chose not to see the destruction. Joyce was by herself. During that time, she and her husband also adopted a young boy who suffered from Fetal Alcohol Syndrome.

The drinking and violence continued for five years. One day, Joyce said: No more. She left, taking her children with her. This abrupt change made her husband realize that he needed to make a choice, and he made the right one. Joyce supported him in his struggle to heal and gain control over his addictions.

Throughout her life, Joyce has been the mainstay for all of those around her. She has helped educate and raise all of her sisters and their children. As a teacher, she touched more than a thousand children. Joyce has also given to her community whenever she was asked, and a lot of times when she wasn't. Many neighbours have been on the receiving end of mysterious gifts of baked goods and home-sewn items. Upon retirement from teaching, Joyce went to work with the RCMP as a matron, once again nurturing those who needed it the most.

Approximately a year ago, her husband was in a near-fatal car accident, lying in a coma for three weeks and requiring continuous care. Joyce once again stepped up. She has stayed with him during the last year, helping him to learn how to walk and talk again, fighting for services that he needs to survive. He will never be the man he was—their lives have been irrevocably changed—yet she stays and loves him.

Through all of this, the shining light in Joyce's life has been her grandchildren. She takes great pride in all that they do, and works hard to ensure that they have all that they need. There are nine grandchildren from three of her children. All of them have special talents, and she celebrates them all. She is especially proud of those who have worked hard to meet a goal, no matter how small.

Joyce's children have always been able to go to her in times of struggle and celebration. She has helped one daughter through a painful divorce, another through the struggles with her children's health, and another with the struggles of infertility. She has worked hard to see that her son has a normal life, and supported his children when he was not able to. She has expected the best of her children, and does everything in her power to support them.

I know that if you were to pass Joyce on the street, you probably would not even notice her. In my eyes, and in the eyes of her other children and extended family, Joyce is a hero. I am proud to call her my mother.

> *Carmyn Block works as an adult literacy coordinator in High River, Alberta. Married with two children, she says she submitted this story because she believes her mother, Joyce, is a "wonderful example of strength and quiet courage." Carmyn says she strives to "live up to the example she has set for my siblings and me."*

⌗   ⌗   ⌗   ⌗

Words of Comfort

JO-ANN JOYCE BELLEROSE

Dear young lady,

I understand that you have suffered abuse and you are hurting. Abuse can be physical, mental, emotional, or spiritual, and worse, all of these. Abuse affects every part of our souls, our appearance, and our self-esteem. Our lives, the lives of our children, and all parties involved are affected because of abuse.

I too suffered in a physically, emotionally, and spiritually abusive relationship. After a fight, I had a black eye and bruises. Everything hurt—from the inside out. I knew that this relationship wasn't healthy and that I had to put it to an end. I decided that I could not let my children see me looking like that ever again. I also realized that my children would be affected negatively. I did not want to damage their futures, or their future relationships.

As I reflect, I know that the abuse was caused by feelings of jealousy, anger, and my partner's need or want to control me. The controlling ways included telling me how to dress, how to wear my hair, even as far as to tell me whom I could speak to. As an outgoing person, I couldn't handle or accept that kind of control.

The breaking point came when I couldn't go to work with my black eye and hurting soul. There was no way that I wanted people to see me in that condition. I missed about a week and a half of work until my bruises weren't so visible. Finally, I gathered the strength and determination to end that unhealthy relationship.

I firmly believe that life is about choices. It is only for you to decide whom you want to live with, where you live, and where you will go from this point onward. You must decide how you want to present yourself to the world.

After meeting a woman who obviously had received numerous beatings, apparent by her appearance, I asked my mom why she looked like that and my mom said, "Don't let a man beat you, because that's how you will have scars, wrinkles, and broken teeth". That scared me, especially the part about the wrinkles! At forty-three years old, despite my salt-and-pepper hair,

I've been told that I look younger. I am reminded of my mom's advice, and my decision not to be abused and to always care about my appearance.

There is a saying that the world is a stage, and we all wear masks. This could have different interpretations. One possibility is that as each of us face each day, we determine which face or mask we will wear for that day, be it happy, sad, grouchy, or mad. This could also mean that though our face may indicate that we are happy, that may not be the case underneath. We might be hurting. . . .

I would like to share a poem that I have memorized and that has helped me live my life.

> Life is like a path
> Of freshly fallen snow
> Be careful how you tread it
> For every step will show.
> —Author Unknown

My dear young lady, my advice to you would be like this:

Care and love yourself, children, and family enough to get out of any abusive situation. Life is tough enough to live without people being mean or cruel to each other. Remember that it is from us that children learn to live, so please be strong and break the vicious cycle of violence that has plagued mankind for generations.

It is your choice or decision to do something positive with your life. Should the decision involve making changes, then go for it. Take that chance.

Think about how you present yourself and your attitude daily. Be aware that first impressions do mean a lot and that, whether we like it or not, people are always looking at or watching us. So love and respect yourself enough to take care of #1, and that is YOU!!

You will find that life does teach some painful lessons, and at times, the road you travel may get a little rocky. However, it is from these very lessons that we gather the strength, the wisdom, and the determination to make a difference in the lives around us.

I hope you decide to make the right decisions or choices so that your life will take on new direction. Always be strong and when you find your-self getting weak, pray for strength and seek strength from those you love, such as your children, family, or friends. Remember, you do matter to those who love you and wish you well, and you are worth a mint to those very same people. Try not to dwell on the past, but look forward to the future—always hoping for better things to come. Try to make every day count in the things you do, what you say to others, and how you run your life. Continue to hope and dream, because hopes and dreams can become reality. It is only for you to decide.

In closing, I wish you grace, peace, harmony, and understanding, and remember:

Live well
Laugh often
Love much
In sisterhood,
Jo-Ann Joyce Bellerose

Jo-Ann Joyce Bellerose is a former councillor of the Driftpile First Nation in northern Alberta. She has studied business as well as child and youth care, and is now pursuing her bachelor's degree in education. "I enjoy reading, writing, gardening, singing, camping, hunting, fishing, and serving my people."

❁ ❁ ❁ ❁

Gratitude
MARSHA ELLEN MEIDOW

To those who tried to break me:
You lost
To those who never left my side:
We won

■■ *Marsha Ellen Meidow overcame severe abuse and addiction to grad-uate from university with an honours degree in women's studies. She works as a youth counselor at the YWCA's Safe Haven program for girls at risk in Calgary. Speaking to girls in crisis, she says: "No matter how horrific your past experiences have been, you can always overcome it. And no matter how alone you feel, you are never, ever alone because you have yourself. That's something that's taken me years to learn."*

⊠ ⊠ ⊠ ⊠

A Morning with a Friend

SUE JOHNSTONE

Yesterday she destroyed the pansies in the front yard. I approach cautiously, although I know that she has regretted it, apologized, and made amends. *Some days are better than others*, they tell me. Today she rises early. Drowsily cheerful, she tiptoes out of her room, waves hello, retreats back under the covers for another few minutes.

I start to run the bath, bubbles rising to the top. She pokes her head in, runs to the linen closet, brings me a towel.

"Please," she signs. "Bath."

"Of course," I reply.

She dips her toe gingerly—not too hot. A sigh as she sinks under the water, closes her eyes. Morning routine. I pour coffee from the machine, focus on the dripping liquid. Weary, I remind myself that we start over every day. Today is not yesterday. Today begins with coffee and a bath. She has forgiven me in the past for not understanding, for making mistakes. I will do the same.

Labels? Reading through book after book of files, they leap off the pages. *Autistic tendencies. Violent behaviours. Erratic. Irrational. Non-verbal. Low intelligence quotient.* Part of her story is told in thick, official medical jargon. Read between the lines. *Physical. Sexual. Emotional. Abuse. Experimental treatment. Electroshock therapy. Institution.*

Even without the books, I could read the scars, still visible under the rose-scented bubbles. Does she think about scars? Shapes across her body. Shapes across her spirit?

She emerges at last, to take my hand. We go to the cupboard, and she digs inside until she finds what she needs—a shiny red hair dryer. She settles into a chair, signs again—"Please." Her face turns to feel the stream of warm air. She holds the dryer; I style with the brush she pushes into my hand. I wonder as I watch her eyes close, as I brush her thick black hair, when was the last time I felt that much joy?

She rummages through a drawer full of makeup containers. Her hair is now windswept and styled. She flips it like a runway model as we inspect the bottles, potions, and colours. Someone has given her lipstick, blush, eye shadow, face powder. The choosing is important. She remembers what it was like not to have that right. Denied a voice in institutions and patriarchy, she fiercely decides even the smallest things now. She tests the limits, changing her mind quickly to see what might happen, still surprised to find that it is okay to change her mind.

I line her dark eyes with kohl. Sage for the lids. She fills a brush with Peach Blossom powder, rubs it on her cheeks and over the bridge of her nose, giggling at her reflection.

Carefully we select from the reds, pinks, and browns. There is no rush. We test a rose lipstick, return it in favour of another, darker shade. She puts it on, looking intently in the mirror. Purses her lips, applies a little more. She looks again through the tubes, choosing the brightest one. Cadillac Red, it is called.

"You," she signs.

I stand in front of the mirror. The colour isn't me, I think. Too flashy. Too confident. I really don't want to try this; it always comes out wrong. But maybe she knows something I don't know. I slowly line my pale lips with crimson, fill in the bottom, then the top. She grins a rosy grin, Sandstone Pink, then looks at us both in the mirror.

"Beautiful," she signs.

When do we stop remembering our beauty? And how is it that she hasn't forgotten? In spite of the scars and labels and betrayal, she has something I don't have. Not the simple joy that many people attribute to those with disabilities, but a desire to find the beautiful. She feels it with her toes when testing the bath water, smells it in the fresh coffee, hears it on her favourite easy-listening radio station. I begin to notice these things more when I am with her.

I can't help but wonder. What would my life story be if I had a book like hers? Would doctors speak above my head, attach me to disorders, prescribe something for my faults? Would they whisper to my friends— *Some days are better than others*—when I expressed anger or frustration? Would I lose my right to choose?

We dance in circles on the living room carpet. Her eyes are closed, and I close mine, too. In the darkness, she takes my hand and twirls underneath my arms. Our bare feet make swirling patterns that look to me like freedom.

> ✂ *Sue Johnstone says she is honoured "to be inspired by several people with autism." The Edmonton writer seeks out "places of security and acceptance where individuals and communities can express themselves." Sue has not named the woman in this story due to her life circumstances and difficulties with verbal expression.*

❁ ❁ ❁ ❁

A Knock at the Door
DARLENE DONALD

It was a very cold night in November. As I was the mother of four sons, I had been doing my usual housework, because I never seemed to have time during the day. I decided to sit down and have a cigarette and a coffee before turning in for the night.

Sitting there, I thought I heard a faint knock at the front door. Not wanting to answer the door at 2:00 AM, I peeked around the drapes and saw an adult and two children. I opened the door, turned on the light, and saw my sister-in-law's best friend. She stood there like a deer caught in the headlights, her two children equally frightened. Her long, light-brown hair was frozen on the sides from the cold; her hands were white. She was wearing an old winter jacket that had seen better days, but wore no scarf or gloves. The children wore mitts, but their little faces were red from the cold, and they were silently crying. They had walked about a mile in the cold.

I brought them in. She was a mess. I gave her a big hug, and told her to go in the bathroom and clean herself up. I took the children and quickly gave them a warm bath, put them into my boys' pajamas, and tucked them into bed with two of our boys. Gave them hugs, and told them everything would be alright. They went to sleep right away, poor dears.

I made coffee. Ellen came and sat at the kitchen table with me. She thanked me for putting the children to sleep. There was complete silence while we drank coffee. She chain-smoked, her hands shaking. I eventually asked if she was ready to talk about what happened. She nodded, tears flowing again, sobbing. "Please don't call the police," she said. Wayne had told her he would kill her if she ever told anyone. I assured her that I would not call the police. She began by defending Wayne, saying he was a good man, he only beat her when he was drunk. She needed him. She was on welfare, had no education, and couldn't support herself and the kids without him. I asked her if this was something she knew to be true, or was it something he had told her. She agreed it was what he had told her, and she believed it.

"The children need a father," she said. She had been raised with five siblings and a mother on welfare. She naturally wanted a better life for her kids. On this night, he had lost his job because he had taken time off work to take her to the doctor. He would not allow her to go out without him, ever. He started beating on the boy because the child wasn't his. When she interfered, he began beating her and kicking her. He finally got tired, and lay down on the couch and fell asleep. She and the kids sneaked out, and walked to our place, hoping to find safety. "I can't do this anymore," she said. "I'm afraid he will kill me or one of the kids."

I hugged her and told her she could stay with us. If she did stay, I said there would have to be some rules. "You will not have contact with Wayne while you're staying here," I said. "You must see your social worker and get some counselling. Look at upgrading your schooling. You will be required to pay room and board. Try to find something you would like to do as a career to support your kids."

I also explained that I had just gone back to school, and was attending NAIT three nights a week. She could help me by babysitting on those nights. This arrangement would have to be discussed with my husband, Allen, but I thought he would be in agreement. She hugged me, thanking me over and over again.

Wayne came over one evening. He just wanted to talk to her for a minute, he said. They were in the kitchen. The TV was on, so I couldn't hear what they were saying. It got very quiet. I got up and went into the kitchen. There was Ellen, cowering between the stove and the wall, and he was standing above her, his fist clenched and ready to hit her. I let a scream out of me that would have woken the dead. I grabbed a frying pan from the stove and raised it to hit him. He ducked under me and ran out the front door. Later the police arrested him for causing a disturbance. We never saw him again. I have no idea what motivated me to do what I did. He was a very large man. However, my temper took over. I strongly explained to Ellen that at no time do you cower to anyone, or allow someone to control you in any way.

Ellen stayed with us for three years. That time was good for both of us. She was a tremendous help to me, doing whatever she felt needed to be done. She turned out to be a wonderful cook. She had tough times— a lack of self-esteem was her biggest problem—but she made it, and did very well. She took academic upgrading, and took a course to become a nursing attendant. Today she is working in a nursing home on Vancouver Island. Her children have hit some bumps on the road, but have turned out okay. After many years, Ellen married a really nice husband who accepted the kids as his own.

I realized through this experience just how lucky I am. Women are not to be pitied, but rather celebrated for the strength we have to survive. It is wonderful to have a partner in life, but only if that partner is willing to see you as a whole person, and believe in you. Women must stand up for what they believe in.

Now retired, Darlene Donald of Edmonton enjoys writing in her spare time. She is a firm believer in the kind of friendship that goes the distance.

⊞ ⊞ ⊞ ⊞

Best Friends
CRYSTAL

She must have felt there was no way out. She cried to me on the phone one day that she felt like a hungry, wild animal that had been trapped inside a cage. I spent many hours on the phone with her. I consoled her broken heart, and told her that there was a better life for her out there, but she needed to get out of the relationship, soon, before something really bad happened to her.

She told me she didn't want to call her parents and tell them they were right about him. She had an iron will that wouldn't let her admit there was a problem. I imagine that she tried everything within her power to make that relationship work. She is one of those kinds of people that refuse to give in without a fight. . . .

I was really worried about her. If I didn't hear from her at least twice a day, I worried. I didn't call her, though. He might have been home, and that would have caused more problems for her in the long run. She called me whenever she could. When she knew he wasn't going to be home for awhile, she invited me over. As soon as his van was in the driveway, I was gone. I never cared much for him and he knew it, too. I told him once what I thought of him, and I was banned from coming over to see her. I told her I knew of a place that she and her son could go. . . .

She finally asked me over the phone one day if I would go to the store and get some boxes for her. My heart skipped a beat. Had all my talking paid off? I wasn't going to press the issue. I felt it might scare her off. I went straight to the store and picked up boxes for her. I waited for her phone call. The wait was excruciating. Minutes seemed like hours. I wanted her to succeed in life, but she was going nowhere with this joker.

Finally I got the call. "Can you come over?" Her voice was heavy with grief. "I need to talk."

I was over there in a flash. I brought the boxes into the house and she was in a panic. "Did the neighbours see you bring those in?" she asked. Her face was full of fear. Her makeup was smudged, her mascara was running, her hair was a rat's nest, and she smelled like she'd slept in a dumpster. I told her the neighbours were working. Her lack of sleep had made her thinking foggy. She told me she needed to get out of there. She'd had enough. . . .

Before I left, she asked me if she phoned at an unusual hour, and I was home, would I come over? I said that wasn't a problem. I went home that night wondering what she meant. Little did I know, I'd find out soon. A few hours later, she called. "I need you!" she said. Her voice sounded frightened. The phone was cut off. I tried calling her back, but she didn't answer. I was shocked and sick to my stomach. The phone rang again. It was her mother, crying: "I just got a call from my daughter. That good-for-nothing wants to hurt my baby!" I told her to call the police. "I'm going over there," I said. "Be careful!" she advised.

I went speeding over to my friend's place. The police were just getting there as I pulled in, and her father wasn't far behind. We all went in, and found her gasping for breath. She was having a panic attack. I took her boy, and put him in my car and waited. She packed a few clothes. One police officer took her aside and told her that she didn't need this kind of stuff in her life. She was a good kid, and needed a fresh start. I think that talk from him did more good for her than she realized. I took her and her son to that safe place where she stayed for a month.

She and her son started over in a new town. I think that she's a strong young lady and she will go far in life. She is in a relationship now where she can do what she loves to do. Her partner gives her all the support and love that she and her child need and deserve. She has accomplished so much. She is going after her goals in her personal life, and with her career. She has a lot going for her, and I am very proud of her.

❖ Crystal, the abused woman at the centre of this story, decided to write from the perspective of the close friend who helped her escape her ordeal.

"My story," she says, "is inspired by my own life, and having to make a decision between living with old choices or gaining experience in a new life. Having a friend in this type of situation is key. She was my lifeline." Crystal lives in a town in central Alberta.

⊞ ⊞ ⊞ ⊞

The Women's Shelter

KY PERRAUN

The itinerant escort who shares my room
in the shelter twists strands of artificial hair
'round her own as she smokes, manic chatter
moving the blue haze enveloping her scarred body.

The skin infection of small children oozes
golden crusts as they run through the room.

I listen in silence, sending telepathic messages
to the bruised mother meditating on the washing machine
the rhythm of laundry the metre of my thought.

Tonight we are making Indian tacos. Rachel
bought two packages of cigarettes. We feel rich
and are safe.

My computer is connected to the universe.
My messages are stolen from the screen.
Help is on the way.

Edmonton poet ky perraun has published her writing in the chapbook Prayers and Graffiti, *in broadsheets, and on audiotapes. Her writing has also been broadcast on radio and television. "I have schizo-*

*affective disorder, and spent time in a women's shelter when I was in
an acute phase," she says. She thanks Alberta's shelter movement "for
providing me with food and shelter when I was unable to care for
myself. I have also experienced violence in relationships, but I am currently fortunate to be in a loving relationship."*

❈   ❈   ❈   ❈

Sandy
COLETTE MANDIN

I don't know anyone who has overcome as much adversity in her life as
Sandy Clark of Calgary. She has survived domestic violence and attempted
murder at the hands of her ex-husband; multiple surgeries to repair her
shot and stabbed body; post-traumatic stress disorder; and, recently, a
double mastectomy due to breast cancer. She is missing an eye, parts of
her sinuses, jaw joints, multiple organs, and now her breasts.

She has survived all of this with courage, a wicked sense of humour,
and an unfailing desire to do the right thing, with loving attention to
family and friends.

When she went into the hospital for breast cancer surgery in the summer of 2003, her daughter assembled an album of writings by friends to
support her mother through yet another difficult time.

Here is what I submitted:

Those who know and love Sandy, I'm sure, are all kindred spirits on
earth.

I love her sense of humour that sometimes has us doubled over in
gales of laughter, reaching for our panty liners. I love how her face warms,
and her smile widens with pride, when she talks about her life mate Rick
and all the fun things they do, about her children and especially her
grandchildren.

I love how she fiercely stands her ground like a little blonde pit bull
when she is defending the hurt, and her sense of fair play.

I love her bad eyeball jokes.

Sandy has taught me more than she will ever know about courage in the face of adversity; strength when there seems none to tap from; humour when I am feeling humourless; persistence, and sticking to my guns when I am ambivalent; instinct, and how to trust my intuition; standing my ground when I know I am morally right; and faith in the face of disappointment.

We know that Sandy is not the most diplomatic person in the world, but she is honest and candid, and I always know where I stand with her. Sandy is my friend and mentor. We have shed many tears together, and shared many laughs. I hope they continue until we can have walker races in an old peoples' club.

 *Colette Mandin lives in Edmonton, where she wrote this tribute to her friend, Sandy Clark.*

❈ ❈ ❈ ❈

Rest in Peace

THERESA JEBEAUX

Dedicated to Hilda Harper and Nisha Prokash

I gotta get my girls
Out of the ghetto
Cause we ain't
No silly ass ho's
We work hard
For everything we got
Whether it's stolen or not
We've done Mickey Mouse crimes
We did our time
We always stuck together

And watched our backs

You'll find us
In the back alleys
Drinkin' smokin' crack
The cops don't scare us
Instead they're scared of me
I just laugh it off
Hangin' with my homies
Cause when times get rough
They're always around
This way,
That way
Up and down
If there's a problem
Come and see me
You know me as the Queen
Miss VIP
We'll hang and shoot the shit
Kill a few beers I promise this
There's always tomorrow
And a few years

To all the girls
Who died along the way
Deepest respect
That's all I have to say

It's hard to bury them
One by one
Listen to me
This ain't no fun

Theresa Darlene Jebeaux, thirty-two, grew up in foster homes and institutions in Edmonton. "In most of these homes, I was molested and *raped," she says. "I turned towards violence, crime, and prostitution. I've lived on the streets for many years, pulling tricks to feed my habit of drugs and alcohol." She says she is in "the process of recovering from her addictions and getting proper treatment" for her medical conditions. She is HIV positive, has hepatitis C, and has been diagnosed as schizophrenic. "Even though I may struggle through this process daily, I can sit back and smile, for I am a survivor," she says. "The poem was written for the ones who didn't survive, and the ones who are still out there, surviving. Thank you for reading my poem."*

⊠   ⊠   ⊠   ⊠

Compassion Came My Way

LYNN HERBACH CRISTINI

God began to reveal Himself in ways I could understand: The planned suicide was interrupted by the unexpected phone call of a friend, both wise and perceptive; the Big Brother, made to measure by prayer, for my son; the co-operative efforts of school counsellors and teachers on behalf of my children; the sincere, respectful love and monetary support of the priests, friends, and parents; the box of apples and the pail of carrots from the neighbours; the anonymous gift of cash in the mailbox; the little brown teapot from the lady next door, whose life of hell met and surpassed mine; the spirit of freedom that poverty brings; and the courage that grows from humour. . . . I began to know that compassion, lived and shared, is the very skin of God. . . .

     Lynn Herbach Cristini is a retired Edmonton woman with a blended family of four children and six "absolutely wonderful" grandchildren.
    "I'm floating, for the time being, upon a quiet, gentle pond—a welcome lull in the upstream swim of my life. Even so, I am certain that my swim is just one among millions, and so I submit my little article in humble response to my daughter's promptings. . . . There are days, even

now, when the pain creeps through. For a while then, the memories touch my soul. . . . But now, in the arms of love and the heart of God, it is safe to embrace the pain. The physical presence and sharing with my husband encourages this freedom. I have come to know Jesus in the flesh, His most humble form. Now, in my life there is love and forgiveness to meet the pain when it comes through."

❊ ❊ ❊ ❊

Find a Lifeline

CORINNE MUDIE

Thank goodness there is help out there for women who are mistreated, disrespected, and unloved. I have found countless lifelines: one of the most rewarding has been the women's support group I attend. We have made friendships, and have been given important information. The most valuable quality is that the leaders have shown all of us support and caring by listening to us, talking to us, and asking us how they can help. Most important, they show us a new respect, something none of us has ever had before from our significant others. By showing us respect, they are teaching us what we need to demand from ourselves and from others!

My courage comes from listening to these women's stories, those that have already left the life they knew, and have lived to tell about it. It was very hard for them too, yet they did it. They all say they are happier, and they only wish they'd done it sooner.

So I say to everyone: Here I am. My running shoes and backpack are on, but my pack is not quite filled yet. Soon, very soon, I will climb. I am looking for that meadow at the bottom of the mountain.

Have faith, hope, and courage.

❊ *Corinne Mudie of Edmonton started this story in 2002. She is happy to report that her backpack is now full. She adds, "Someone recently asked me, 'Where do you find hope?' I said that I find my hope in God. That is still my answer, yet I realize I also have found a new hope within myself. . . . I know that strength lives deep within me. We all have the power to pull it up out of ourselves and use it to make us stronger, to get us through another day."*

Corinne says her own life experiences have been draining and scary. "I persevere knowing that I have a whole new life waiting for me, one of happiness and devoid of fear. I have learned that there are good men out there."

⊞   ⊞   ⊞   ⊞

Thank You, Edna

PENNEY QUWEK LEBLANC

This is a true story about my "leg up" woman, Edna Pugh, who was my safe place, and my calm in the storm as I struggled to grow up in southern Alberta. The remarkable thing about her influence on my life is that she wasn't even related to me, but became the mother I never had.

I come from a thrice broken home of eleven children all told. Fighting, arguing, yelling, criticizing, and physical violence marked all relationships in my family. My biological mother deserted us when I was nine years old. I lived with my father, and I was eventually expected to look after the five kids who ranged in age from five to eleven. My father remarried, when I was twelve, to a schizophrenic woman with two children of her own. She jumped ship with them, dragging us through a nasty divorce when I was fifteen. Twice in my young life, babies I had loved and looked after were ripped from my arms to go with mothers who didn't love nearly as much as I did. My father has since remarried and divorced again.

Through all of this terrible time, I cherished the times I got to see Edna and be part of her family.

My first trip to the farm owned by Edna and her husband near Dorothy, Alberta, was at the tender age of three months old. I slept in a dresser drawer, as there was no crib for me. Edna taught me to tie my shoes, cook well, and survive the chaotic life I was forced to live through. Life on their farm was not easy. The days started early and if I got up early enough, I got to spend more time doing the chores with Edna's husband, who I called Papa. After chores I could help in the house, or go out and help Papa some more. There was always plenty of work to do, and mouths to feed, but along with the work there was much laughter, love, and soul nourishment. It was the only place in my horrific world where I felt special, safe, and like I mattered.

Edna listened to my stories and let me pour out my feelings, and she filled in the blanks with the things I was too ashamed of, or afraid to speak about. She helped me see that the choices my mother made were not directed at me personally. They were only about her. She had many nuggets of advice she shared with me:

All children are a blessing

Be frugal and know the difference between wants and needs

How to love and be loved

To be happy doing a job the best way you can

Make work fun: crank up the tunes, or talk to someone to distract
    you from the chore at hand

You are special

You have a life purpose, and you are of value to society

Pretty is from the inside out

Edna doted on me, listened to all my woes, acknowledged my feelings, and gave me solutions where I thought I had none. Through it all she never told me what I should do. She always respected me enough to let me make the choices for myself, even when she would have made different choices. I was made to feel like one of her own.

Edna passed away quite peacefully at the age of seventy-nine in Yuma, Arizona. She was a snowbird who loved to spend the winters of her final years there. When she passed away, it was as though my anchor in life went with her. . . . Going back to the ranch after the funeral, Papa introduced me as his daughter. I felt like a kid back on the farm again, and my heart swelled with pride.

Writing this has been hard for me. It is not easy to let her go. As I remembered I cried, laughed, and rejoiced. She left me a rich heritage of common sense, advice, love, and acceptance. The things she taught me, and the love she generously shared with me, have left a profound mark on my life. I endeavour to apply the lessons she taught me, and keep the door of my home open to those who are lost in their lives—as she did for me. She was truly my mother in every sense of the word, even though she did not give birth to me. There is not a day that goes by that I don't thank God for what she taught me, and that she was there for me.

Penney Quwek LeBlanc lives in the Lloydminster area, where her family raises cattle. "We may not all have a 'leg up person' in our lives, but I was truly blessed to have one," she writes. "I strive to be one to those who come into my life in need—just as Edna would have done." Penney is proud to use the same brand as Edna did on her cattle: -X7.

⊞   ⊞   ⊞   ⊞

The Comfort of My Culture

KIM GHOSTKEEPER

When I left home I made a promise to myself that I would not live this way. Things were going to be different for me, but change was painful, and change was hard. I felt so much guilt about leaving my family. I worried for my mother's safety. I couldn't see how she would end the violence. I wanted her to quit drinking, if that would solve the problems, but she did not have the strength to let go of alcohol.

Life was different for me. When I left home I began to learn and experience the strength of my cultural roots. My first and subsequent jobs in those early days were with Aboriginal organizations. I began to know more and more Aboriginal people. I felt included in the community. When I moved to Edmonton, it was like discovering my long-lost relatives. I don't know how it came to be, but I was introduced to the Friendship Centre, which in those early days was a gathering sport for a lot of Aboriginal people who lived in the city. I became a regular at the sober weekend dances, even though I had never been a drinker. They were great social events where kids and elders, teens and adults gathered. During these dances everyone danced together, and young people like me were taught to dance the two-step and old-time waltz. In return I became a regular volunteer with the Friendship Centre, and met many other people.

I found a community that understood my pain and shame. It was a community willing to take me in, and teach me about my culture and heritage. I was accepted. I even got into an Aboriginal training program, partnered with a community college, and I got a diploma. My parents were so proud of me. They had never considered the possibility that I would go past high school, which in itself had been a difficult but major accomplishment. . . . Through the program, I attended cultural training, which exposed me to traditional teachings and history about Aboriginal people.

I came to see the life of my parents from a whole different perspective. I became more compassionate when I learned about the residential school experience, knowing my mother had gone to residential school. I appreciated her separation from the north, the overwhelming culture shock of the city, from a whole new perspective. At the end of the course I returned home and for the first time in my life, I talked, really talked, to my mom. Many subjects were too raw for her to talk about, but she was willing to open up about some.

I was twenty-one when I went home to help my family with my mom's funeral. The trouble had started with a few drinks with friends down at the bar, and continued with a few more drinks around the kitchen table. After the friends went to bed, my parents started to argue. It escalated. The friends were startled by the sound of gunshots. When George came out of the bedroom, he said he saw my mother with the rifle pointed at the floor. My dad was down; he had taken a bullet to the leg, but was still alive. George got his wife out of the house, and ran to the neighbours to call the police. By the time they arrived, it was too late. She had barricaded herself in a back bedroom, and seated on the footboard of the bed, she leaned over a rifle barrel and shot herself in the heart. My dad sustained a gunshot wound to the main artery in his upper leg, and almost died from blood loss. Our family sustained a major trauma, and we were scarred, each in different ways, for the rest of our lives.

They say that when an Aboriginal person commits suicide, their spirit goes to the northern lights. For our mother, we can only hope her spirit has found a safe and accepting place, knowing that her children have broken the cycle of violence.

Kim Ghostkeeper says she now comprehends the domestic violence she witnessed as a child. "My mom was from the North, and once married, was disconnected from her family, her community, and her culture. My dad had grown up in a violent household himself, and had left home very young to take jobs in the mining industry. It was a tough world of hard drinking, tough talk, and physical work. They were young parents who were drowning in responsibilities, obligations, debt, and the sober reality that they were two people trying to make a go of it, and that they were not emotionally equipped to do it." Kim is a project management consultant in Edmonton.

❋ ❋ ❋ ❋

The Friend Behind Me

TAMMY DAY

With some counselling and someone who cared about me, I started to make inroads to understand why I allowed certain situations to occur in my life. I had someone behind me saying, "You can do it. I have faith in you." Slowly I began to believe that message above all the others that pulled me under. It was not easy at first, but with rock-solid support I moved forward, inch by inch. I moved backwards sometimes too, and I disappointed myself deeply. Still, that person behind me said, "You can do it. I have faith in you." I picked myself up and continued the journey. I started to realize that life is not about achievement, and being perfect, or being everything to everyone. It is about just being who I am.

Tammy Day is studying part-time for her Bachelor of Education degree at the University of Alberta, while also raising her two daughters. She works full-time and writes in her spare time. She says she would like to encourage all women who doubt themselves to look deep inside and remember who they are and how they make a difference.

"The road so far, as rocky as it has been, has enabled me to become who I am now. Understanding that I have options, and making better choices, allowed me to become what I was meant to be—a successful woman."

❁ ❁ ❁ ❁

I Remember the Power of a Few Words

CINDY TOKER

One day, in order to avoid a beating, I left the house. My sister-in-law called the local women's shelter. I had never heard of a women's shelter before that day. I got to the shelter and stayed for a couple of days. One of the workers told me: "You will only be abused as long you allow it to happen."

I was surprised to hear this, because I felt I had no power over my own life anymore. I spent a few days in the shelter and went back to my husband. The words of this shelter worker never left my mind.

My husband and I moved around, following work, and always hoping that things would be better in the next place. Each time we moved, I would try to find out where the nearest shelter was, just in case I needed to go there. I managed at times to get counselling through local shelters before we would move on to another town. The words that the counsellors spoke—empowerment, encouragement, and hope—were so foreign to me that they were like another language. I listened. I kept mulling these words over and over in my mind.

It was now the summer of 1988, and we moved once again. I had been with my husband for eleven years. His rages were relentless now, and it took next to nothing to set him off. I was in constant fear. Our lives were chaos. I was tired. I was beaten. I wanted it to end. I was terrified to end it.

Just before Christmas 1988, I received a beating that lasted all night long. It was severe, it was continuous, and it was deadly. I thought that my life would end that night. I eventually got away with the kids. I was nearly blinded by black eyes, but I got out. I was determined that day that I would never go back.

There was no women's shelter near where we lived then, so I managed to find friends and family to house me until I healed. The bruises eventually healed, and the children and I went on with our lives. My husband tried for a long time to talk me into going back to him, but I never did.

Eventually, there was a women's shelter built in a town close to mine. I no longer needed to run to a shelter, but it was comforting for me to know that it was in the area. I often thought about women who were still living what I had lived and left. I hoped that they would go to the shelter for help.

I lived as a single mom for a number of years. It was a hard life but a happy life; we did not live in constant fear anymore. I went to college in 1993. I met a kind and decent man whom I married in 1994. My children are all adults now. We have a good life.

A few years ago I had the opportunity to apply for part-time work at the local women's shelter. I met the workers, and marvelled at their patience and strength when dealing with women who are trying to put their lives back together. The workers listen to each story with concern and care. I have watched these workers empower women, and I have tried to follow their example. I have listened to their words, and I have watched women respond to their words.

I remember the first beating I received. I remember the last beating I received. I remember the first words ever spoken to me by a shelter worker. I remember the power those words gave me.

I will always be grateful to that worker a long time ago.

The women whose enduring patience and kindness help women leave the chaos and terror of abuse will always be my heroes.

This story is dedicated to my friends and coworkers at the Peace River Regional Women's Shelter. I have learned so much from all of you.

Cindy Toker lives in northern Alberta. After leaving an abusive marriage, she worked part-time as a Crisis Intervention Worker at a women's shelter. *"My heart will always be with the shelter and with the workers who help women in need every day."*

❁ ❁ ❁ ❁

To Somebody

MARJORIE BRUNO-WHALEN

I just wanted to write you this letter to let you know that I love you. We may not know one another, and we may never even see one another, but I just wanted you to know that you are loved.

⊠ *Marjorie Bruno-Whalen lives in Edmonton. "I am a forty-five-year-old First Nations woman, a mother of five. I have raised a very beautiful granddaughter since (her) birth." She offers this message for women who are still living with the domestic abuse she left behind: "Take the first step to peace, and remember there are some good people out there to help you. Only you can take the first step. Prayers to the victims."*

❁ ❁ ❁ ❁

Start Building a Home

MARY ANNE LEHMAN

I left when I realized that the abuse was not going away. . . . The decision would affect the rest of our lives for better or worse, but it was a decision that the kids and I made together. We decided to leave, and we promised to work together to make a better home. Over the next ten years, the kids and I learned the following things.

Start building a home the day you leave. Home is where we can laugh, sleep, and, most important, feel safe. A home has nothing to do with the bricks and mortar. It has to do with how you and your family feel.

Work together as a family. Even the smallest child can have a job and some responsibility. Children do not understand the full ramifications of what is happening, but they do know what is happening. Give them a job to do, and they feel they are positively contributing to your new home.

Don't promise your kids what you can't give them. Promise them a better life with a little more laughter, if you all work together.

You cannot control what happens to you. Bad things happen to good people. You can control how you react to the situation. You can knuckle under, or you can fight and move on! Accept responsibility for your decisions and your life, and your children's safety.

Guilt is a useless emotion. If it is not constructive, let it go.

Homemade presents are best. They show love, and they don't cost a lot.

Perspective is everything. If you think your life will improve, it will—with hard work and commitment. If you think things can't change, things will not. *You are in charge.* Change your world and lead your children forward.

Children follow a parent's example. They learn not by what we say, but by what we do. Just because there is violence in a child's past, it does not have to be in his or her future. As I learned to cope, my children learned to cope. As I learned to believe in my abilities, my children learned to believe in their abilities. As I improved my skill levels, so my children improved theirs. As each day passed, we moved forward. The kids and I both learned to cope, and believe in ourselves. We gradually learned to succeed in life.

Sometimes the best things in life are free: a tea party, a teddy bear picnic, playing at the park, going to the library, walking along the river bank, and especially rolling in a pile of leaves in the fall.

Finally, the hardest lesson that we learned—and we are still learning it—is to take one day at a time. Some days are good, and some days suck. Move forward, because going back is not a choice.

Last but not least, we realize that having lived in a violent home changed our lives forever. There are days when I get angry that the kids and I had to see the violence, feel it and experience it. It wasn't fair. Yet it was an experience. It is in the past, and we have to move forward. We cannot change the past. We can only learn from it and grow. With the kids, I just explain that their father was responsible for his decisions, and we are responsible for ours. We are lucky because we know we can make good decisions under pressure. We finally know we did not cause the violence. We were victims but we survived, and we will succeed with whatever life sends us. We know it's not what happened that defines us; it's how we handle the situation, and the decisions we make. We know our purpose is to make our individual world a place of peace, sleep, and satisfaction.

One day at a time, we put it behind us. One day at a time, we move forward.

Mary Anne Lehmann lives in Calgary, where she enjoys reading, quilting, gardening—and her loving family. "It's very hard to make the decision to leave a violent home," she acknowledges. "Sometimes we look for someone who can fix our situation for us. Nobody else can do that. We have to fix it for ourselves."

❀ ❀ ❀ ❀

Find Peace and Comfort in Nature

LIZ LISTER

We as humans have become far removed from our ancestors, not only in time and space, but also in consciousness. Unlike them, we can neither understand nor respect nature and its many powers.

If you separate yourself from nature, you have denied your very source. When we neglect our physical, emotional, and spiritual health, as we try desperately to keep pace with a world that consistently outruns us, we find ourselves increasingly at the mercy of the technology we created to serve us.

When we reconnect with nature, we become conscious of our true sense of strength and peace. The earth nourishes us. The air rejuvenates us. The water cleanses us. The stillness calms us. All of this is what we have forgotten.

Take more time to reconnect with nature in your life. When you go for a walk, fine-tune all of your senses to the sights, sounds, smells, and textures around you. Feel the solid strength of the tree, the richness of the earth, the softness of the grass, the freshness in the air. See everything in nature with reverent eyes, and feel yourself become *alive*. Embrace your connection to the universal life force.

⊞ *Liz Lister wrote several pieces for the* Standing Together *project while staying at the Women's Emergency Accommodation Centre in Edmonton. "The director brought me all the information regarding this book," she writes. "A little shy, but inspired by the staff to enter, here I am. Enjoy my work." Elizabeth says her life story is "much more complex than needs to be revealed. Living on my own since I was fourteen, a ward of the Children's Aid until I was twenty-one, I have been in and out of institutions to deal with the compounding issues which have plagued my entire existence." Her problems include abuse in several forms. She says her life today is rich with "friends, love, laughter, and hope." Her lifelong motto is: "If you can't be good, be great."*

⊞　⊞　⊞　⊞

Never Lose Faith in Yourself

CHERIE TRAHAN

You are the one, in the end, to hold yourself up
Don't let anyone empty your cup
Believe in your spirit, keep your cup full
Try to reach for every goal
You can do it if you're in charge
For it is your life. Live it large
You are beautiful inside and out
No matter what anyone says
It's how you feel that counts
Forever and always, believe in yourself
Trust in the Lord

This is an excerpt from Cherie Trahan's longer poem about recovery from domestic violence. She writes, "For three and a half years, I lived with his drugs and his physical and mental abuse. Every time I left, he hunted me like I was an animal. He broke into every house I rented to try and get away from him. He would hold me captive, and lock me in rooms.

"I felt like I could write forever about not letting go of your spirit, to not give into the darkness . . . . I pray my words will hold someone up and encourage her that her life can go on." Cherie began a new life after her abusive partner died. She and her new partner, Rob, are raising their two children in Stettler. To staff members at women's shelters, she writes, "Thank you and God bless you for all the work you do. You are angels on earth."

❁ ❁ ❁ ❁

Remember, You Are Worth It

CHRISTINA HILLIER

Don't ever allow someone to run you down. If you do, then they will continue doing it until the end. If you think you deserve that, then you can expect it to continue. Stand up for yourself. Fight for yourself. You are no longer a child. You have a voice. It needs to be heard. Don't keep your feelings hidden. Express yourself. You count. You matter. . . .

If you don't allow others to treat you badly, then you have won. You have rights. Please love yourself, and try to forgive yourself for your weaknesses so that you can move forward and grow. Most of all, forgive those who trespass against you. In order to recover, you must forgive, and then never look back. If you keep looking behind you, you can't see what's ahead.

What's ahead is great! You have to envision it, and believe you deserve it. It will happen for you.

Christina Hillier writes:"My desire to share my story, is to help someone realize we can't change our past, or choose our parents or the outside influences that we've experienced. However, we can change our perspective and our future. . . . Thank you for the opportunity to share my story with others. It acts as a reminder to myself to live one day at a time. One baby step at a time."

❋ ❋ ❋ ❋

Laughter Helps, Too

KERRY "KONDO KLUTZ"

Kondo Klutz screamed in panicked pain as her
practiced ass careened onto the open dishwasher
bruising both ego and elbow as excruciating agony
spread like heated knitting needles down her arm

scathed memories of a two-inch gash, gouged Klutz's butt flesh
as she cried and pulled herself up from the ceramic tiles
no one heard or saw the clamour except her valourous cat
whose raucous screetch matched her own startled cry.

Weeks later, damaged nerve endings still persist as
she goes about her daily duties haphazardly knocking
ass and elbow at each awkward turn, while staring
at the black and yellow queen bee coloured elbow

Dishwasher door repaired, dishes cleared away
she bandages the past memories
in which the Kondo Klutz takes a fall to the nth degree
and updates her resume to stunt woman status

Kerry "Kondo Klutz" is the pen name of a Calgary woman who describes herself as "a retired wife, former seamstress and secretary. She shares a condo with Cilla, a fat white cat with lemon-lime eyes and half a tail. Kerry enjoys sharing her funny poems, prose, and recipes "over the techno tablecloth." She decided to begin an independent life at the age of fifty-six, after thirty-three years of marriage.

She writes, "I go forth continuing to face the challenges of living on my own. Writing my story, including some of my cathartic poetry, helps me through the loneliness and emotional pain." Humour, she says, is always a big help.

⌗ ⌗ ⌗ ⌗

Write Away the Hurt
ELLIE MCGAUGHEY

I discovered in my mid-thirties that I was able to release all of my inner emotions through a pen, rather than towards another human being. It has been, and always will be, my own personal therapy program. When anxiety sets in for whatever reason, whether it be happy or sad, I write. The best part is that I don't have to share these thoughts with anyone if I choose not to. There was a time for me that was extremely dark, and through my own words I was my own saviour. When I sat back, and actually read what my real thoughts were, life became just a bit less challenging. It is my time to truly be at one with myself.

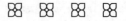 *Like many contributors to* Standing Together, *Ellie McGaughey writes of the contentment she has found with a peaceful man, and her gratitude to friends and family members who stood by her through the difficult times. Today she lives a happy life with her family in a town north of Edmonton. An excerpt of her poem, "And Then There was Peace," appears in the next chapter.*

⊞ ⊞ ⊞ ⊞

Cellphone Safety
VICTORIA STEADER

I got a cellphone on the advice of the police during my divorce actions. I have kept this phone because my children still worry about me when I am out, because of all of my ex-husband's threats after I left him. I do not buy extras, so that I can afford to pay for cellphones for both of my children, and for myself. I believe it is invaluable for all women to have a cellphone for safety purposes, and I wish there could be some type of funding available for this, or alternately, that cellphone companies would supply cheap cellphones for women that they would only use when their safety was at stake.

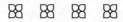 *Victoria Steader is the pen name of a woman who lives in central Alberta.*

⊞ ⊞ ⊞ ⊞

Where I Am Now

❈ ❈ ❈ ❈

Renewed Life

KY PERRAUN

My lover returns from the world with a bouquet
and meal. He reads my poem
with a red pencil, shaves the odd word
but preserves most lines

After dinner he composes music
and I swallow my medicine

The wooden desk, the pale chrysanthemums
the beautiful concoctions that steady the mind.
His skin, my heart, this life
like a phoenix flying into the future
with no room for remorse

All phantoms banished to books
our bed strewn with new memories
of tenderness, lucidity and love.

> *Edmonton poet ky perraun wrote this poem as the concluding seg-
ment of her longer descriptive piece called "Shattered Looking Glass."*

So Now, I Am Getting Over It

MORRIGAN

Not all of my experiences are included in this story, as some are too
painful, embarrassing, and just too humiliating to write about. When
someone tells you that it is not your fault, you are not responsible for his
or her actions, how do you believe that to be true, when you cannot figure out why it happened?

I thank my counsellor for her understanding and patience. The knowledge she has shared with me has helped me begin to know myself. I now understand that the things that happened to me as a child helped shape who I am, and made me vulnerable to experiences I had. I now know that the people who abused me did so because of who they were, and not because of anything that was wrong with me, and I deserved better.

I also thank the women's shelter staff for their knowledge. So now I am getting over it. I keep myself safe. Although each morning I wake up wondering if today is the day that he goes through with his threats, I try not to think about the gesture of a gun, or the comments he still makes when he feels he has the opportunity. The police have assured me that if he has not done anything by now, he probably will not. I try not to get upset, even though he has everything that I worked so hard to obtain. I try to remind myself that I am not the only one who has to go to the food bank.

I challenge my thoughts when I feel a sense of shame and humiliation when I accept the generosity of other people in order to have the basic necessities of life. I have days when I think about the negative and vengeful things I could have done to others. Sometimes, through my pain and anger, I wonder what would happen if I did to him what he threatens to do to me. Would I be "smart" enough to get away, or would I push it and try to take out the lawyer, too? Where would it end? Who should be held responsible? These feelings are short-lived and come when I am feeling overwhelmed with life.

I am so thankful that I had a nervous breakdown instead. Without that breakdown, I would not have met the two people who helped me learn that I am not responsible for anyone else's action, but I am responsible for my reaction.

It has taken me a long time to learn that knowledge is power. I still have a long way to go in my healing and in my legal pursuits, which are ongoing after three years, with no clear end in sight. But I know my story will have a successful conclusion, because each passing day I become stronger in myself.

I have the confidence to know that even if he follows through with his threats, and gets me today or two years from now, he no longer has power and control over me.

Morrigan is a pen name. The author was born in Europe, and grew up in a large family. "I was brought up in the generation where women obeyed their men. Unfortunately, the men in my life have been unworthy of that kind of power. Through an abusive father, husband, and common-law partner, I have learned that no person shall ever rule over me again." She now lives in southern Alberta.

❀ ❀ ❀ ❀

Running

KATE DENIS

Running
From a past determined to hold on
Pushing and pulling
I get up to be dragged down
Beliefs, thought long gone,
Ghosts that haunt me
Hidden beneath the surface
Will this struggle ever end?
Stuck between the worlds
Won't go back
Afraid to move forward

Taking a deep breath,
I open the door
Welcoming the experience
Of a soft touch
A warm embrace
An affectionate smile
Wanting desperately to believe it
Fear suffocates me
Wounds swallow me whole
Projecting a cold heart

Better to push away
Some fantasy in my head
It's not real

Uncomfortable in my own skin
Scared that my feelings will betray me
I toss and turn
I fidget and flinch
Recalling the burn of previous times
The threat of violence
Punishing silence
Gave away my soul once before
Wanting to open up to something more
So easy to drown in my loneliness
Buried by my misery
Nothing is worth this pain

If my blinded eyes could only see
The person standing in front of me
Nothing left to pretend
Seeking patience and understanding
Healing old scars that have begun to bleed
Time creeps on
Longing for connection
I climb the walls of my self-made prison

Finding what was lost
I break free from the shackles that bind me
Limitless possibilities
Not sure where the next step will lead
No reference point to cling to.

I pick myself up
Running forward
Everything I've ever wanted
Lies before me.

"Running" is an excerpt from a series of poems that Kate Denis contributed to Standing Together. *Her poem "Empty" appears in the second chapter.*

❈ ❈ ❈ ❈

Giving Back
IRENE HAIRE

I wanted to help people with sexual abuse issues, so I went back to the University of Alberta for a BA with a major in psychology and a minor in art. My future ambition is to be a counsellor for women and men who have been sexually abused. I want to help and maybe pay back what was successfully given to me. It feels so fantastic to finally feel good enough. The world feels like my personal stage. I learned another valuable lesson. I am no longer afraid to try anything, and I know I can do what ever I decide to do.

❈ *Irene Haire of Edmonton is a pharmacist who has contended with childhood sexual abuse. "The more we talk about these problems in our society, the more awareness and healing will take place. That is my greatest wish."*

❈ ❈ ❈ ❈

And Then There Was Peace
ELLIE MCGAUGHEY

Then by chance, or by fate, a stranger enters her life
someone who recognizes the elusive signs, whatever those were,
and the black began to appear as gray, then turning to white,

it becomes easier, with each meeting, to explain how she feels
her words and thoughts suddenly begin to make sense
countless tears are shed as she learns to mend her torn soul
but now she knows there will be peace to follow

then another stranger appears, but this one different
this one accepts her unconditionally,
then loves her, and wants her to share his life;
and her children witness the rebirth of their mother
with undying love, once lost
the family and friends, feared gone, hold their arms wide open
and then there was peace!

Ellie McGaughey has rediscovered contentment with her family in a town north of Edmonton.

⊠   ⊠   ⊠   ⊠

Trusting Again

L. CITY

What would sex be like with another man? The world seemed cold-hearted at times, when new friends abandoned me. I finally met someone special, but didn't recognize it at first. Love came in an unexpected package, but finally the veil lifted from my eyes, and I recognized what was before me: a true friend.

I love happy endings, but life isn't over. I take each day as it comes, never knowing what lies ahead, never trusting that happiness will last. But thank God for today. As the sun rises predictably each morning, so love daily warms my life and blesses my soul. Who could ask for more than that?

L. City is the pen name of an artist who is rebuilding her life in Red Deer.

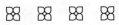

Life Changes

ELSIE GARSTAD-LAMBERT

One to get ready
Two to get set
Three to go . . .
And here I go again

Here I go—running away—to Salmon Arm
Down the road again
May 8th
Justice of the Peace this time
My word! Three times!
A friend asked me, when I voiced my uneasiness,
"Would you rather the family members, nieces and nephews, say:
'I have this aunt who has been married three times!'
or
'I have this aunt who has been living with this guy for three years
and she's pushing seventy!'"
Why, of course, my choice would be the former.
Do I care what people say?
Hmm, maybe, but only just a smidgen

He has eased his way through the stone wall of my heart
Has made my life worthwhile with hope
Plans for the future and joy in my heart

He is my Prince Charming
He is my Third Time Lucky
His name is Jack.

Elsie Garstad-Lambert grew up in east central Alberta, and now lives in Edmonton. She was divorced twice, and a single mother for many years, before she met Jack in 1996. They married in 2001. Elsie wrote Oilpatch Recollections: The Way Things Were *to commemorate the*

fiftieth anniversary of the oil discovery near Leduc, Alberta. She divides
her time between family life and writing projects. She says she is thank-
ful that she "found the courage to overcome my fears, and learned to trust
and love again."

⌘ ⌘ ⌘ ⌘

Willpower
ANONYMOUS

My son was born in 2003. When I was at the hospital, shortly after his delivery, three social workers came to see me, due to my past history with child welfare. I was given the opportunity to share with them my journey towards change, and to tell them the steps I had taken in order to be a healthy parent to this child. They are also considering letting me raise my daughter who was taken at birth.

I have continued walking without looking back. It has been very hard, but I am not alone. I have a lot of support that I am grateful for, because I don't know what I would have done, or where I would have gone, otherwise.

I have pulled myself through all the destruction in my life by seeking help through various supports, including Alcoholics Anonymous, second-stage housing for women leaving domestic violence, and counselling through a number of agencies.

I am very happy in my life right now. I have finally given myself the opportunity to discover who I am, and to learn my potential as a person and as a mother. I am doing things that I never imagined I would be doing, and I can finally say that I enjoy life, free of drugs and alcohol. I have learned to respect myself, and to only allow people into my life if they will respect me and my wishes.

I learned that if you have the willpower and willingness to change, you can achieve this. I am at a much different place in my life that I was two years ago. I am still working on a number of goals that I have set for myself, and as I reach these, I will continue to set others. This is a lifelong journey that I am proud to say I have begun.

The author of this story chooses to remain anonymous. After leaving a violent partner in Calgary to seek refuge in a shelter, she is rebuilding her life in a new home. Born in northern Ontario, she has been living in Alberta for nine years.

⌗ ⌗ ⌗ ⌗

A Flower Blooms
MARILEE LESKIW

Beneath the burdens of life
A flower blooms

Though beat and bruised
From struggle
She broke through
The crust of rubble

Her strength holds
Her head high
She is no longer tormented
By the things gone by.

Her smile tells you
She's passed the test of success

She preserved through pain
She took her life back again

She continues to give
She continues to live

And so a flower blooms.

Marilee Leskiw of Edmonton has put abuse behind her with difficulty. She says she has learned that black eyes, bruised arms, and broken bones "heal up and go away," but other kinds of abuse are harder to forget. "The abuse words, they stay in my head, and on my heart." Adopted as a child, she is exploring her Blackfoot ancestry through her art. Marilee thanks a counsellor named Carol and a women's support group in Mill Woods, in Edmonton, for helping her to begin a new life. She dedicates this poem to her two sons.

❈ ❈ ❈ ❈

Crazyhorse Girl

JOAN WHITE CALF

I've changed my name, and celebrate native spirituality, and get around pretty damned good in the big city. I have gone to college in the pursuit of higher learning. I have learned to appreciate my body and realize my assets. I'm a risk-taker and a daredevil, not a "dumb girl." I've returned to a lifestyle that has kept me alive and happy, when before all I could see and feel were the spirit killers.

Horses are my job once again. I am a fifty-year-old bandana-wearing woman who gets to greet her equine charges every morning with terms of endearment like, "Okay kidlets, who wants a face massage?" I dance in front of them, and encourage their rapt, relaxed attention with baby talk and satire. I go home at the end of the day to a beautiful little bungalow in the country, surrounded by trees and birds. I have a good car, and do exactly as I please. I shy away from naysayers and chronic complainers. I enjoy peace and happiness, and feel truly fortunate to be here. When I run low, and need a little help, I let my pissed-off side take over. Moments later I have a plan to address my stressful thing, and then I take a fighting breath and let time carry me on.

❈ *Joan White Calf spent much of her childhood in east central Alberta, but now lives in Edmonton. She has worked as a lounge waitress, horse trainer, wildlife rehabilitation worker, and a lay counsellor in a women's shelter. She enjoys walking, mountain biking, watching foreign movies from the library, and fine Alberta horses. To women in abusive relationships who are enduring violence or humiliation, she says, "Do not be fooled for one second. Other people's reality might not have anything to do with you. Get out!"*

❁ ❁ ❁ ❁

Tar Pits

OLGA COSTOPOULOS

I'm afraid that if my demons leave me,
my angels will desert me, too.
                    —Rainer Maria Rilke

The needles are losing their efficacy
The doctor has suggested hypnosis
"to free the ch'i blocked by childhood trauma."
Can those tar pits be siphoned out?

And could the attendant demons then
collect unemployment insurance?
Or would they just dig new depressions
In the sponge that calls itself a brain?

Might my angel then call for reinforcements
who would come trooping in, white wings a-jostle
to clean the place and earn their keep
by fending off the demons?

Or, if it were that easy, could one say,
sotto voice, "Magic Time," pass a hand

in front of the face and carry on
like an actor, knowing precisely
where the lights are, but acknowledging
only what lies beyond them?

❖ *Olga Costopoulos teaches creative writing at the University of Alberta in Edmonton. Her writing has appeared in many journals in Canada, the US, and Australia. She published a collection of poems,* Muskox and Goat Songs, *in 1996.*

❖ ❖ ❖ ❖

I Graduated at Sixty-Five

KAY LONG

I wrote, meditated, and finally came to the realization that 'I' was no longer part of a 'we'. The dreams and goals that my husband and I had shared would no longer work for me. I had to decide what I planned to do with the rest of my life. I vowed that I would spend the balance of my life helping women who had experienced trauma from either widowhood or abuse.

To accomplish this would mean going back to college to complete my education. I knew that life experience alone would not get me where I planned to go. I also needed those letters behind my name. Within five months of my release (from hospital), I put the farm up for sale, bought a small house in the city, and moved away from all that had been so dear to me for so many years. The most important things I took with me: the happy memories, the farm dog, and two orange tabby cats.

Going back to school after forty years was almost more of a challenge than I could handle, but I was determined to carry through with my newly formed goals. I was amazed that my classmates and professors were so accepting and helpful to the old fossil who joined them in the hallowed halls of learning. The most frustrating part was trying to retain what I studied, with a sixty-plus-year-old brain. I was enthralled with the academic world, especially philosophy, literature, and sociology. Somewhere along the way, I discovered that I was meant to be a social worker. The reality was that I had actually operated as a social worker for many years, without the title or the degree. My co-workers in northern Alberta had often referred to me as a bleeding heart. Today I understand that I was just seeing the world through a social worker's eyes.

Finally, at the age of sixty-five, when most people retire from the workforce, I graduated, and began working part-time as a facilitator for women's groups. Working with women who have endured such difficulties from domestic violence makes me stronger in my conviction to help find a solution to this major social problem. I enjoy the work I do, and I learn so much from the clients. I will continue to work as long as I can. At this time and place in my life, I am proud to join the ranks of Carl Jung's "wounded healers."

Both Carl Rogers and Erik Erikson, masters in the field of psychology, ultimately gave the same answers to the question: What is the secret to a happy old age? Each of these theorists of the psyche, in his own way, arrived at the same conclusions: One must help other people, and one must release the artist that is in everyone.

Today I am doing my best to help other women who have also endured and survived abuse in their lives, so I have found half of the way to a happy old age. Since I am already a published writer, I am saving oil painting for my senior, senior years!

Born in Oregon, Kay Long left a violent and abusive marriage early in her life. She moved to Canada with her second husband in 1970. Together they built a log home, and a happy life, near Lesser Slave Lake in northern Alberta where Kay worked for the provincial government. Widowed at fifty-nine, Kay moved to Edmonton to attend college and university. To be closer to her family, she recently moved to Lethbridge where she is developing a counseling program for couples in crisis. She dedicates this story to Ann Maksymiw and the Stop Abuse in Families Society in St. Albert.

Winter Sunrise

NAOMI DEUTEKOM

Winter sunrise
Shimmers above the horizon.
Golden reds, pinks, and orange
Tinge the clouds
Lighter hues paint the snow
As coloured light bounces back from the surface

Cold, dark
The night has been
Hungry tendrils gripping tight
The deep, cold dark of winter
Gives way, unwillingly,
To light

Grief, pain, deep sorrow
Hold our souls in the night
Like the winter sunrise we can't be held.
Grief lets go.
Hope and love shimmer on our souls
Our hearts live again.

Naomi Deutekom is married to Don, her husband and friend of twenty-two years, and is the mother of two teenage boys. She has run her own business, worked in the retail trade, and returned to school as an adult. She has also worked as an adjunct faculty member at a Bible college, and is now the Family and Community Support Services Coordinator for the town of Sexsmith in northern Alberta.

Describing her recovery from childhood sexual abuse, she writes, "We do not have to remain victims. We do not have to hide from life. We can live it. We can have joy, peace, and confidence. Not only can we overcome the past, but we can use it to grow and develop, allowing us to become the individuals we want to be."

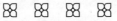

Looking Back, Looking Forward

CECILY MILLS

A phone call. My ex-husband died this morning in Kelowna. I felt sorry for him, sorry that he had died still as angry and bitter as the day he discovered that I had ceased to be his possession.

Thirteen years ago, after two years of a heart-wrenching search for answers, I packed my car—still in his name—and drove away from the Edmonton home I had lived in for seventeen years. Belgravia Road, Fox Drive, Whitemud, Yellowhead Highway, Kamloops, Vernon. Eleven hours. Next day, Kelowna, Penticton, Osoyoos, US border, Seattle. Ten hours.

I would have come back if he had given me a sign—any sign at all—that he understood my decision, that he was ready to compromise. Instead, he sealed his fate by declaring: "The problem is that I gave you too much freedom."

Even before I put the phone down on the day he died, I felt immensely relieved that I had decided to leave him so long ago. I pictured myself as having stayed in the marriage, and then finally being released. I saw myself as a bee, so long imprisoned in a bottle, that she is incapable of flying out once the jar is open. I pictured myself as a browbeaten sixty-five-year-old woman, imprisoned in a dungeon of low self-esteem and fear.

How different the outcome because of the decision I had made thirteen years earlier! Today I am a vibrant sixty-five-year-old woman who decided at the beginning of 2003 to celebrate each and every day of the year. Those thirteen years of freedom I claimed for myself opened the doors to adventures I had not even dreamed of. I worked as a full-time volunteer in a shelter in Seattle. I volunteered seven years in Central America. I learned Spanish and some Q'eqchi. I laughed and cried with my Edmonton ESL students, young and old alike. I travelled, camped, hiked, skied, volunteered, made new friends, bought a condo. Most important, I did what I wanted. No one told me what to do. No one criticized me, or put me down. . . . I can continue to make life-giving decisions for myself, and for women struggling to make their dreams come true.

Cecily Mills was born in Quebec, and moved to Alberta in 1969 to study at the University of Alberta. After a long career as a high school teacher, she began a new life as a full-time volunteer in 1990. She enjoys hiking, camping, travelling, and writing. She lives in Edmonton.

❁ ❁ ❁ ❁

Gifts to Me

ANN HARRINGTON

The pain is deeply felt until I sleep
The days are busy, at night I weep
Abandonment at such a time of need
Has left me feeling lonely
The life within me I soon will hold
The remainder of my love will unfold
The love to be given will be shared by three
These gifts from God are presents to me
My mind and body move at a weary pace
In time, all will fall into place.

Ann Harrington wrote this poem when she was six months pregnant with her third child and her husband had just left the family. After suffering severe postpartum depression, she slowly rebuilt her life. A former volunteer with the Family Centre in Edmonton, Ann helped other young mothers cope with postpartum depression. She says she is grateful for the help her family has received from the Big Brothers and Big Sisters organization. "I believe from first-hand experience that we live in the best city in the world," she writes. "My passion for writing has always been a saving grace."

❁ ❁ ❁ ❁

Bad Can Be Turned into Good

ANNA BRANCH-WAGER

From the day my father was convicted of sexually assaulting my younger sister and me, to the day he died, I waited for him to acknowledge his guilt. It never happened. In many ways this lack of remorse affected me more than the abuse itself. I kept wondering if I had been wrong, if I had somehow misunderstood what had happened.

In those days, sexual abuse, incest, or spousal assault weren't talked about. This silence often resulted in the victims believing that their situation was unusual. It wasn't until I became an adult that I realized my experience was, unfortunately, all too common.

Since then I have become a survivor. I believe my past has made me more sensitive to others. I am aware that a smiling face can often mask a painful life. I have also become strong enough to trust others, and this has resulted in a happy marriage to a wonderful man. I have achieved many things in my life, including a stint as a civic politician, and being a published writer. Would I have done these things anyway? I don't know. I do know bad can be turned into good, or as George Meredith says, "There is nothing the body suffers which the soul may not profit by."

> *Anna Branch-Wager is a specialist in driver education in Edmonton. She moved to Alberta in 1991 from Ontario, where she was the founding director of a women's shelter. She was also one of the first female city bus drivers and highway coach drivers in Orillia, Ontario. To other girls and women who have experienced sexual abuse, she writes, "Remember that you are a special person. Don't let anyone, or anything, take that from you."*

⊠ ⊠ ⊠ ⊠

Who am I?

R. HENNING

I'm proud,
I'm hardworking
I'm a good person, I know

I've learned a lot about life
But most of all I know
I'll make your life brighter
Because of my strife

Sometimes, when I feel that I haven't accomplished a lot,
I look to my children,
So happy and free,
And see what a child is meant to be!

For I've accomplished so much,
The greatest of all,
I'm a mother and a person you see

Through my children, I show
That even though my past is a part of me
I will still grow

My accomplishments are shown
Through my children, you see,
For they are the *greatest* part of me!

Look at me!
Who am I?
I'm just proud to be me!

R. Henning is the pen name of a Calgary woman who has struggled to overcome the effects of profound childhood abuse. This is an excerpt from her longer poem, "That Girl." Henning says the wounded girl in the poem has grown up to be "a proud wife and mother of two children, who knows how important it is for people to do the best they can at whatever they're doing." She thanks the social services agencies that helped her when she was in need, and encourages other people to end the violence in their lives.

⌘ ⌘ ⌘ ⌘

I Have Recovered

DOLORES THERIEN

One day, the man of my dreams—Number Two—managed to shoot me in the back with a double-barrelled shotgun. He even had the nerve to pull both triggers. The reason? Does it even matter? All I know is that he called me the next morning to do his banking for him. Oh, he did jail time, and has chosen to leave me and my children alone, for which we are grateful each day.

I still, to this day, don't get it. What makes any abuser think we will just pick up where we left off before the abuse? You know what I think the answer is? It's *us*. We give our abusers the go-ahead for another round, each and every time we let them back into our lives. I like to call it the Letting Them Back In Syndrome. It is simply no longer open for discussion for me. I will *never, ever* have this syndrome again.

Where are we now? My children and I have gone through a number of community-based programs, receiving guidance and counselling to help us cope with the trauma of me being shot, as well as other types of violence and abuse we have experienced in our home. I have recovered from my physical and mental wounds, and I have evolved into a more self-confident and strong woman. I endeavour to help other women who are experiencing troubles at home, whether it be by providing just a kind word, an ear, or advice about the agencies that can help them and their children.

I have survived. I have overcome. I will continue to persevere. My life is an open book, and if I can help anybody out there to understand that they *can* get out, I am there for them!

> **❈** *Dolores Therien, who describes herself as "a strong Métis woman," has worked as a government employee in Alberta for twenty-two years. The mother of two sons, she has written a longer story about her experiences with severe childhood sexual abuse and domestic violence in several relationships. "My story, like thousands of Alberta women, began at a very young age," she writes. "I, of course, lived with this secret for way too many years." She says the secrecy about abuse will need to end before progress can be made.*

❈ ❈ ❈ ❈

You Can Do It
M.G.

I was seven the first time I was raped
I was eight and full of hate
I was nine, and it still happened all the time
I was ten, and I wanted it all to end
I was eleven and it just kept happening again and again
I was twelve when I took a bunch of pills, cut my wrists . . .
I felt there was nowhere to run, nowhere to hide
I couldn't sit there and watch my whole life go by. . . .
I'm thirty-six now, married and bright
I work all day but I'm home at night
I've been through good, I've been through bad
I've been happy and I've been sad
But with my life now, I can say I'm really glad
I once heard a saying:
Whatever doesn't kill you, will make you stronger,
This I believe, as I'm still here, and I plan on staying a lot longer

In one's life you have to set goals
You can do it, as I did
At the age of twenty-five, I went back to college
and I became a palliative care nurse
My name is on a plaque at the college
for an outstanding-student award.
I raised my kids, straight through, and went to school.
Remember:
Whatever you put in your heart as a goal, you can do it.
You will be fine.

 *M.G. lives in Edmonton. "Thank you for taking the time to listen,"*
she writes.

❈ ❈ ❈ ❈

Of Tapestries and Grief

HEATHER PLAIZIER

Her surface
a rich tapestry
colours, texture, talent, vibration

Her soul
hidden depths
echoing
a bottomless pit of need

At least the dragon
says it's gone
Says it isn't a dragon
anymore

But I'm so used to brushing up
against its fiery breath

Getting singed
scalded
scorched
severely burned

And now it's gone
Is it?
and I'm supposed to revert
thankfully
to a place of balance
and trust

Thank you but
my guard
will stay up

Grief forestalled
by onslaught

Bombardment over?

Now I cry

(bring)

in peace

 *Heather Plaizier submitted a cycle of poems to* Standing Together *about "first, the joy of a relationship with a woman, then surviving and getting out of what became a destructive relationship." This is the concluding segment. Raised on a farm in the Peace River country, Heather began her career as a teacher. She now works in the field of immigrant adult education and social services in Edmonton. She says she hopes that all of the writing in this book will provide "inspiration or insight to others, but also extra steps of healing, reclaiming personal strength, and ownership of our own courage."*

❁ ❁ ❁ ❁

Talking to the Abuser

IRENE KONEV

What demons chased you?
I'll never know
Was it delusions?
Or outright lies?
Those things you'd "seen"
With your own eyes.
It doesn't matter anymore
Not anymore
I've kept my sanity and my soul
And dignity is mine alone
I rise from the ashes and the gore.
I have no house, but I have a home.
The more you've taken, the more I'll own.
I shall prevail and persist,
Live, and no longer be in remiss.
Yes! You did have trust
And trust you broke.

Irene Konev wrote this poem after leaving a violent relationship eight years ago. She raised her seven children as a single parent while she worked with abused women and children. "I hope this poem makes a difference to someone who needs to hear about abuse and know that it can be overcome," she writes. "Don't worry too much about your children. They are more resilient and powerful than you might realize. When mine grew up, they thanked me for getting them out of a destructive home."

�֍ �֍ ✷ ✷

Prayer to a Lost Love

HEATHER KING

Last night you came to visit in my dreams
As we embraced, the fallout of our past was all erased, or so it seems.
You wanted me to know that all the lies, and the black eyes,
you would undo
Not to change the course of destiny,
only to prove to me your love was true.

In my dream I felt no need to fix the past
The shackles bound around your heart and soul, you shed at last.
We faced each other in a place and time
where all was clearly understood.
No twisted sense of shame, no need to blame, no bitter pain
Just clean and good.

That I felt no sense of loss did not seem strange
That I'd offered up myself as a sacrifice a million times
to see you change.
That our love had not been strong enough, or deep, or long enough to
    rescue you.
But strong enough for us to say goodbye,
to let me go and start anew.

May your painted pony's stride be swift and strong
And the pathways that you travel lead you home.
May you wake each day to find the joy and promises within.
May you know that I have forgiven you.
Amen.

> Heather King works with Child and Family Services in Grande
> Prairie. At home, she enjoys her artwork and raising horses. She volun-
> teers with a therapeutic riding program and hopes to combine her love
> of people, art, horses, and the outdoors when she retires. "In my own

process of healing, I have often wondered where this all began," she writes, "and as I watch my daughter struggle with her search for peace, I wonder where will it end?"

❁   ❁   ❁   ❁

Standing Together

❀ ❀ ❀ ❀

An Afterword

JAN REIMER

You have just finished reading unforgettable stories and poems that honour the bravery in a woman's heart. I hope this book will encourage readers to stand beside all people who are enduring domestic violence and abuse in their lives. If we work together, I believe we can confront the problem, and defeat it.

Perhaps you picked up this book because you are struggling to overcome violence or abuse in your own life. I want to acknowledge your courage, your worth, and your dignity. Remember that all of the women who contributed stories and poems to this book—and many, many others besides—stand beside you as you read these words. We admire your determination to search for a more peaceful and rewarding life. We understand that things can go wrong, and that you might stumble and fall many times on the difficult path to a better future. If you fall, we know you will stand up again. You will keep moving forward. We are amazed at your strength, your endurance, and your ability to get through the challenges of a single day. In the toughest hours of your toughest day, listen to the voices of the invisible friends in this book. Can you hear us? We are cheering you on. You can make a better life for yourself, we are saying. We respect you. We believe in you.

Perhaps you searched for this book because you are deeply worried about a member of your family, or a close friend or neighbour. You are frightened for someone who seems to be trapped in an abusive relationship, and has not yet found the will to break free. I hope the stories and poems in this book will remind you of the importance of patience and compassion. Have you recognized the early warning signals? Is one partner's anger out of control? Does the abuser try to control or isolate the person you're worried about? Do you ask yourself questions like: Why does she stay? How can I help? These questions are natural. Listen to the writers in this book, who answer on their own terms. Remember that it is sometimes a brave act to stay, as well as a brave act to leave. A woman will need to make decisions for her own safety, and perhaps for the safety of her children, that you might not understand. She will need to find the confidence and the right time to act. Rather than blaming a woman for staying, hold the abuser accountable instead. Don't make excuses for unacceptable behaviour, or ignore the steady insults and occasional violence that you witness with the hope that both will disappear. Support the woman you're worried about, and her children, as clearly as you can. Offer resources to help her reach a decision. Listen to her with love and concern. Don't judge her or criticize her. Stand beside her.

Perhaps you purchased this book out of simple curiousity, with no experience of domestic violence and abuse in your surroundings. I hope these women's stories—from every age group, every income group, every kind of community—will inform you about the pervasive damage of a crisis in our midst. You don't know anyone who has experienced anything like this? Think again. The problem has been hidden in homes for centuries, and dismissed in the wider society, even laughed at in the House of Commons. We have come a long way in the past decade in acknowledging the severity of different kinds of domestic violence and abuse, yet the problem stubbornly persists. If you don't look for it, you won't see it. It happens in every town and city, in every neighbourhood, in every country in the world. No extended family, no ethnic or religious group, is immune. If you have children, they are playing with abused or bullied children at school. If you have colleagues at work, some will be quietly struggling with the impact of abusive relationships as they try to earn their living. The consequences—the hurt, anger, fear, violence, injuries, and exhaustion—affect all of us, over generations. We need to stand beside the strangers in our community—not only our family members, friends, and neighbours—as they search for a peaceful way of life. Strangers need allies, too.

If you work in the shelter movement, you are already one of those allies. For several years, I have witnessed your hard work, compassion, and commitment to change. Like many people, I admire your dedication and your belief that change is possible. You are often stretched to do your job with limited resources. It isn't easy to leave the heartbreaking stories at the shelter door when you go home after a long shift to your own family. The suffering of other people will travel with you, and sometimes it must be a heavy burden on your shoulders. In Alberta alone, 5,930 women and their 5,558 children sought refuge in shelters last year. Counsellors handled more than 34,000 crisis phone calls. Still, you find the will and the energy to make a difference in the lives of troubled families, often without the recognition you deserve. Read again the appreciative messages from the storytellers who speak through this book. Your words of comfort, and your respect for the dignity of each individual, will be remembered long after you finish your last day's work at the local shelter. Thank you for standing beside women and children at times when they feel abandoned and forgotten. They know they can rely on you. The rest of us do, too.

I anticipate that *Standing Together* will be a source of strength for women who are living in abusive relationships, or leaving them; a source of encouragement for the family members and friends who love them; and a wake-up call for communities. This is our purpose.

The *Standing Together* project began with one woman's great idea. Iris Evans, then Alberta's first Minister of Children's Services, suggested that an inspiring book about women's experiences in Alberta might be a good way to raise funds for the prevention of family violence and bullying in the province. In January of 2003, Iris invited Alberta writer Judy Schultz and me to discuss the idea over lunch at a restaurant in Edmonton. The Alberta Council of Women's Shelters assembled a small team of volunteers to work on the project. The late Lieutenant-Governor Lois Hole agreed to be the honourary patron of the project, and we deeply regret that our dear friend did not live long enough to hold this book in her hands. She would have hugged every writer who delivered a story or poem!

We distributed a Writers Wanted poster to every corner of Alberta: not only to the women's shelters, but also to public libraries, schools, seniors' clubs, colleges, universities, and writers' groups. The poster requested stories and poems that would "celebrate the lives and experiences of women who have struggled with challenges, and yet live rich and joyful lives." We declined fiction and stories that had been published elsewhere.

Soon, the word about *Standing Together* was spreading through personal e-mail lists. We were amazed at the heavy response, and extended the deadline to the spring of 2004 to accommodate as many interested citizens as possible. At this point, we were still anticipating inspiring tributes to both well-known and unfamiliar Alberta women. When we reviewed more than 250 submissions, we found that about 80 per cent of the contributors had addressed the issues around domestic violence and abuse. This did not surprise us, as the Alberta Council of Women's Shelters had sponsored the writing project. Men were welcome to submit a story or poem, but only one did. He was a northern Alberta high school teacher who encouraged a student to submit her story of sexual assault and recovery.

After lengthy discussion, the team decided to honour the wishes of the majority of contributors. We decided *Standing Together* would be a collection of stories and poems about the experience of violence and abuse, and the triumph of moving beyond it. It would be a hopeful book.

We asked each writer to make her own choice about whether to name herself in the book, use a part of her name, a pen name, or remain anonymous to protect her identity. We sought each writer's consent for the final selection; many stories and poems were abbreviated with the authors' permission.

Unfortunately no book is large enough to contain all of the stories and poems submitted to this project. We treasure the entire collection, and with the permission of the authors, we will preserve all submissions in the Provincial Archives of Alberta. Special thanks need to be given to the Standing Together Project Committee: Sheryl Fricke, Linda Goyette, Alyssa Haunholter, Ruth Linka, Patricia Poohachoff, Judy Schultz, Katherine Sheppard, and of course, our Honourary Chair, the woman who started it all: Iris Evans. I would like to thank Alberta Children's Services in particular for its generous support for this project. I think the writers speak to the strength and courage of Alberta's women as we celebrate the centennial of our province in 2005. Even so, the messages in this book are universal. If we listen carefully, we will hear echoes of these words from every part of Canada and the United States, and from every nation around the world.

I believe that we can stand together—and work together—to create a world free of violence and abuse in all of its forms. Will I see it happen in my lifetime? No. Will it happen in the lifetime of my son and daughter? I hope so with all my heart.

Jan Reimer is the Provincial Coordinator of the Alberta Council of Women's Shelters, and a former mayor of Edmonton.

Edmonton writer LINDA GOYETTE selected and compiled the stories and poems in *Standing Together*. She is also the author of *Edmonton in Our Own Words*, a new history of the city, completed with researcher Carolina Roemmich; and *Kidmonton: True Stories of River City Kids*, a companion volume for children. She won the Grant MacEwan Author's Award for this work in 2005. Linda wrote for the *Edmonton Journal* for twenty years as a reporter, editorial writer and editorial page columnist and won two National Newspaper Awards for her writing. She contributes a regular column to *AlbertaViews* magazine, as well as feature articles to regional and national magazines. Her first book, *Second Opinion*, was published in 1998.

THE ALBERTA COUNCIL OF WOMEN'S SHELTERS is a voluntary organization that supports women's shelters and their partners in communities across the province of Alberta in western Canada. The council believes in a world free of violence and abuse, and it pursues this goal with a focus on abused women and their families.

Members believe in the empowerment of women and the equal worth of all people; the importance of working together for change; and the community's shared responsibility to break the cycle of intergenerational violence and abuse.

The council is a determined advocate for its member shelters and their staff members. It works to improve public awareness of domestic violence and abuse; ensure adequate resources for shelters; research and promote improvements in public policy and systems; and encourage professional development for shelter staff.

Alberta has a population of about three million people. Women's shelters regularly accommodate close to 12,000 women and children each year. Sadly, because they are full, shelters turn away almost as many women and children as they serve. Yet each hour more than four women living in fear call Alberta shelters' crisis lines.

The fact is that Alberta leads provincially in domestic violence incidents and deaths. ACWS is committed to ensuring that no death goes unnoticed and to bringing about change to create a province free from violence and abuse. For more information, visit: www.acws.ca.

ACWS
Alberta Council of
Women's Shelters

In Memoriam

⌗ ⌗ ⌗ ⌗

The heart and soul of Alberta doesn't lie in the rich farmland,
the majestic Rockies, the precious oilfields or bustling cities.
As wondrous and important as those features may be . . .
that heart resides in our people.

—Lois Hole, Honourary patron of the *Standing Together* project